SPIRIT-FULL LEADERSHIP

Discovering Your Inner
Guide to Inspire and Lead

Published by Motion Media International
Editors: Parker Hansen, Yasmin Phillips, and Eric Wyman
Cover Design: Motion Media International
Typesetting & Assembly: Motion Media International

Printing: Amazon
Creator: John Spender - Primary Author
Title: *Spirit-full Leadership - Discovering Your Inner Guide to Inspire and Lead*

ISBN Digital: 978-1-925919-77-6
ISBN Print: 978-1-925919-78-3
Subjects: Motivation and Inspiration, Spirituality, Leadership

TABLE OF CONTENTS

—∘⌒⌒∘—

Preface 1

Spirit-Full 5

The Awakening Moment 7

A Free Spirit in a Body 13

The Essence of Spirit-full Leadership 27

Self-Awareness is a Lifestyle 39

Exercising Awakening 45

Universal Truth 49

Breaking Out of the Ordinary World 61

Awaking Spirit-Full Leadership in Us 69

Clarity Is Empowerment 81

Breaking Out 89

Tapping Into Our Spirit 95

A Call for Love 105

Being a Spirit-Full Leader in a Fast-Moving
and Changing World 117

Aligned with Purpose 123

Leadership and Performance 137

Exploring Spirit-Full Leaders 141

Essence of the Spirit-Full Leader 165

Spirit-Full Leadership with God 185

Healing Our Inner World 205

Energy 223

Cultivating Insights and Wisdom 243

Nurturing Spirit-Full Leadership through Mentorship: Cultivating Insights, Wisdom, and Practical Applications....... 249

The Discerning Eye.. 253

Vulnerability and Sensitivity...................................... 257

Author Biographies **261**

Afterword **265**

PREFACE

———⟞०⟝∕⟜⟨०⟞———

I n the vast expanse of leadership media, there exists a realm often overlooked yet profoundly transformative: the domain of spirit-full leadership. Our book, *Spirit-full Leadership: Discovering Your Inner Guide to Inspire and Lead*, illuminates this uncharted territory, offering insights, wisdom, and practical guidance to those who seek to lead from a place of authenticity, compassion, and purpose.

We have come together from diverse backgrounds, bringing our unique perspectives and experiences. Drawing from our years of spiritual exploration and leadership coaching, we have a deep understanding of the inner workings of the human spirit. Through our observations and experiences, we offer a grounded approach to the practical application of spiritual principles.

As we embark on this journey together, it's necessary to acknowledge the context in which this book emerged In a world marked by rapid change, uncertainty, and complexity, the need for visionary leaders who can navigate these turbulent waters with grace and wisdom has never been more pressing. Traditional models of leadership, focused solely on external success metrics, often fail to address the deeper needs of people and organizations.

At the heart of spirit-full leadership lies a simple yet profound truth: the recognition of the interconnectedness of all beings and the acknowledgment of the inherent dignity and worth of every human being. This recognition forms the foundation upon which effective leadership can flourish, fostering environments of trust, collaboration, and innovation.

In the following pages, we invite you to embark on a journey of self-discovery and transformation. We offer a roadmap for reconnecting with your inner guide, the source of wisdom and intuition that resides within each of us. By blending ancient wisdom and modern insights, this book illuminates the path toward becoming a more authentic and purpose-driven leader.

The idea that true leadership begins from within is central to the philosophy of spirit-full leadership. By cultivating self-awareness, empathy, and compassion, leaders can create ripple effects that extend far beyond the confines of their organizations, touching the lives of those they serve and inspiring positive change in the world.

However, this journey is not without its challenges. In a world that often values external achievements over inner growth, the path of spirit-full leadership requires courage, resilience, and a willingness to embrace vulnerability. It is a continual learning and growth journey marked by moments of triumph and struggle.

Yet, precisely through these challenges arise the greatest opportunities for growth and transformation. As you delve into the pages of this book, we encourage you to approach this journey with an open heart and a curious mind, ready to explore new possibilities and discover the limitless potential that resides within you.

In closing, we extend our deepest gratitude to you, the reader, for embarking on this journey with us. May the insights and practices shared in this book guide your path toward becoming a spirit-full leader, inspiring and empowering those around you to reach new heights of excellence and fulfillment.

With Gratitude
John and Stefan

"Leadership is based on a spiritual quality. The power to inspire others to follow."

~ Vince Lombardi

SPIRIT-FULL

LEADERSHIP
Is
the vibration of
LOVE
transformed into a being of
JOY
through the heart, mind, body, and soul of
A HUMAN BEING
manifested as acts of
GENEROSITY
radiated as
APPRECIATION.
Which, by the mere presence,
EMPOWER
those who follow to
generate a **WIN, WIN, WIN** relationship
for
YOU, ME, AND MOTHER EARTH
leaving nothing but a fresh scent of
GRACE

The Awakening Moment

Awakening – to the vibration of love

The lake was still. The forest on the other side of the lake mirrored itself on the water, bathed in the sun's golden and pink embrace. I settled onto a log at the water's edge, submerging my feet and legs into its gentle embrace. On this warm July evening, everything was serene. Birds serenaded the setting sun, their melodies resonating with the stillness within me. Or perhaps it was I who resonated with nature's serenity. I felt an undeniable connection to the vast tapestry of existence. For a fleeting moment, it was as if a lens had widened, capturing a brief snapshot of beauty and momentarily awakening a profound awareness within me.

It stood clear that the mere force behind everything created is love; nothing "natural" is produced by evil. The only energy that exists is love. It's in myself, the lake, the sky, the forest, and the animals. Everyone is created by universal love, not for any reason, just because it's the only pure force. The force loves to manifest itself in a form like a roaring ocean, a warm desert, or a snow-dressed mountain top just because it can, just for the pure joy of manifesting itself.

The camera lens closed, and I was back to "normal." I started to walk back to my friends, but the moment changed me forever. This was one of several enlightening experiences I have had from an early age as a young boy, and it was life-changing.

There was no way back; nothing has ever been the same, regardless of what it has been about: working as a manager, investing, driving motocross, skiing, and being a father, husband, or son. This moment has been like a flashlight on everything I've encountered since—a flashlight of truth, illuminating life's brutal honesty.

While so much opened up in all its beauty, I started to feel a lot of melancholy and became depressed. The sadness of seeing all the beauty and mess humans make of it has sometimes been unbearable, until I found an acceptance in my heart of what is. It can neither be changed by force nor by humbleness lived into a new creation.

Imagine opening a door and standing in the doorway, looking at the world around you with a completely new vision. You see, feel, and experience everything in a new way. It feels amazing; maybe it is a unique, brighter light. Perhaps colors are more vibrant, sounds are more apparent, taste changes, and the breeze feels stronger on your skin. Maybe the sun feels warmer on your skin, too. The blood in your veins starts sprouting like champagne. Your senses change in every way.

Maybe you turn around and look back from where you came. Is that true? Have I been living there? Is that really me? It can't be real. You turn around again, looking out with your new vision. Maybe this feels so good that you think, "I want to stay here forever. This is amazing! I have to tell the whole world about it."

And you keep standing in the doorway, stunned by the experience, and hanging on to it, making it last forever. But then, you realize that neither the old world nor the new is gone. It's been there the whole time. But you feel different within it, and it acts differently toward you.

Awakening is the first step toward experiencing life from an entirely new perspective. Just like waking up in the morning to a new day, you can imagine a plan for the day to come. You will never know the day until you have led yourself through it, the sun has settled, and you have fallen asleep again.

"No one knows the day until the
sun has settled."
- Bengt Jacobsson

Or, just like the first chapter of a book, the awakening is just the teaser that wants you to continue reading. The difference is that there is no last page. To experience the gift of awakening, we have to keep on walking. The road ahead might not be straightforward. It might not always be blissful. That is not the purpose of awakening. The objective is to dissolve the dusty clouds that clutter our minds. To help us bring grace into this world, to our own lives and the lives of others.

The key to continuing a spirit-full journey is moving forward and recognizing and valuing our past experiences. As Winston Churchill wisely remarked, "When you walk through hell, don't park there; keep walking." This sentiment resonates deeply with John and me; we believe it applies equally to moments of pure bliss. Life's essence is transient; we can't cling to or control our first moments of awakening. Instead, we must learn to be present, living each moment fully and cherishing the love and vitality that anchors our existence.

The main thing is not that we walk. The way we walk, think, act, and operate matters. It is the leadership we give ourselves and influence others with. What we occupy ourselves with or, let's say, play with, on the journey is not of concern. It doesn't matter if you are a multimillionaire investor, priest, carpenter, filmmaker, or something else. Awakening does not come from money, religion, politics, education, logic, or statistics. Those are only constructs made up by people. Most of the rules we live by were made up by someone because they thought it helped serve their purpose.

In our modern era, we have the luxury of questioning dogmas and illusions. Instead of adhering strictly to rules made by others, we can innovate and establish a more cooperative way of life for you, me, and Mother Earth.

We have unfolded life's force, "love," in our way in and out of different circumstances. John and I have never met in person, just digitally, but we feel we're on the same wavelength. We share a lot of insights even though we grew up in different parts of the world, thousands of miles apart. Sure, we are two middle-aged, bald white dudes who grew up in Western culture, and we've had the luxury to afford to spend time with ourselves exploring life. But we have both been open-minded to taking in new aspects of ourselves during this time and now we'd like to share these insights and stories with you.

As we write the chapters of our life's story, we must reflect: What narrative do we wish to unfold? Is it our unique rendition of a tale rooted in love?

Our life's journey has brought us to this moment, built on the foundation of our experiences, our choices, and the legacies of those who came before us. This shared history has shaped both of us.

So, what do we aspire for in our next chapter? Of course, the most fundamental choice is to awaken and live a life based on the frequency of love.

The spirit-full leader opens the door, steps into the light, and keeps walking with it, consciously aware of their unawareness. They know they have not discovered the truth to its full extent and possibly never will; it is too vast. Nevertheless, they know and have remembered the mechanics of the art of being a humble human.

Spirit-full leadership means being in alignment with the spirit, soul, mind, and body while at the same time being human. Even though it's a superpower, we're not talking about people who are supermen or superwomen. A spirit-full leader embodies high-level energies, like peace and joy, and brings harmony and clarity to any situation. With their mere presence, they influence others with new perspectives, awareness, and transparency by showing them the way. A spirit-full leader can guide others to awaken, connect, and align stronger with the spirit's full path to be a role model of love.

Life starts with a heartbeat and then a breath and ends with a heartbeat and a breath. Everything in between is the exploration and the experience of being human on earth, enjoying the adventure.

The spirit-full leaders serve as guides for adventure. They are the masters, and they already exist within us. We must let them out.

"**Enlightened leadership is spiritual if we understand spirituality not as some kind of religious dogma or ideology but as the domain of awareness where we experience values like truth, goodness, beauty, love, and compassion, as well as intuition creativity, insight, and focused attention.**"

~ Deepak Chopra

A Free Spirit in a Body

—————⟶o⟨⟩o⟵—————

T hank you to the universe for giving me another day to live this life. I am thankful for the opportunity to create this day as a human being. Please provide me with knowledge, clarity, and common sense to make it a day I will be proud of.

This phrase is the trick for tuning in for the spirit-full leadership daily.

However, the inevitable questions that arise with awakening are: Who am I, what am I, and what am I doing here? Awakening opens the door to a universe beyond our imagination; when it opens and we step into unfamiliar territory, we often enter the zone of not knowing what or who we are, and, most certainly, what we are doing here.

In moments of profound realization, it's tempting to lose oneself in the vastness of spirituality and get lost amidst its intangible heights. Yet, the true challenge lies not in soaring amidst these ethereal clouds but grounding those revelations here on earth, anchoring them deeply within our hearts.

A pivotal moment for me came not from earnest effort or deliberate pursuit. Instead, it was when the teachings I had once heard from a master transformed from mere words into a lived experience. It was a revelation allowed to manifest organically, without force.

This revelation shifted my perspective entirely: We aren't merely humans searching for a spiritual experience. Rather, we are boundless spirits navigating the intricacies of the human journey.

13

Grasping this truth reshaped not only my personal narrative but also the way I lead.

Humans are not an unconscious pile of flesh walking around distracted by the drama of fleeing, feeding, fighting, and fornicating. Even though one could think that sometimes, if they look at the news or themselves. Instead, we are superconscious spirits that come to form, manifested by love, living in the garden of Eden. How well do we use that platform and how well are we aware?

When I experienced, felt, and consciously understood this for the first time, it gave me a whole new vision of life. It was a 360-degree groundbreaking insight. So much fell into place, and I felt at home. In an entirely new light, I could see the beauty in all the small things, the ugliness, and the misconceptions humans live by, including myself. It was a moment when everything came alive for me in a completely new sense.

I had studied so many angles of "spirituality," religion, philosophy, and quantum physics—the old Greek philosophers, the Eastern masters, the Western thinkers, and the Bible. I've also realized that guys like Albert Einstein and Stephen Hawking explained it through physics. It was pretty straightforward; every description turns to a single energy source: love, the pure will to create and to be created.

The life force energy only wants to be loved, used and manifested. We are that energy manifested in a body. The body is a magnificent tool and a home that has been given the power to think, act, and operate extraordinarily on this planet in a way no other creature has been given. We have been given the ability to consciously understand that we are energy and can read and direct energy in a very sophisticated way, and we have been given the power to understand beyond understanding consciously. We have invented art, science, math, psychology, medicine, technology, and philosophy.

Sometimes, we imagine that we must move ourselves to find the answer. But we never have to go anywhere to wake up or discover the energy; we are always home. Wherever we are, we cannot be anything else. It doesn't matter whether we are at our house, sitting in a cave in the Himalayas, or traveling thousands of miles away. We are always with ourselves with our spirit, connected or disconnected. Therefore, the awakening moment is always just around the corner or ever-present. Every situation is a portal to awakening and maturity. We must allow it to happen.

We are free spirits, and having a human experience means we do not have to seek or strive for enlightenment or anything else if that would not be our choice. Enlightenment is already there and has always been there; it's already inside us. Our spirit is already connected with the "source," so we are spirit-full at birth. We never came, and we never went. We can relate to what's already there and build stronger relationships with our spirit. If we like to play with it, we can explore our true nature to open up more of our gifts and uncover the great mystery.

Buddha was enlightened after 49 days of meditation, but he was not enlightened because he meditated for 49 days. It was on the day when he surrendered that he was enlightened. And that's the story for many others, too. It's often after a long struggle that when we give in to the battle and come to peace with it, we level up; we are enlightened to a new level of consciousness. And for every story, there is a new level. It was the same for Nelson Mandela. It's said he was enlightened when he came to peace with his destiny.

A Free Spirit in a Leadership Role

We are not merely here to strive, perform, or chase outcomes. This realization reshaped my perspective on leadership. Previously, I've approached leadership as guiding people toward a specific goal, driving both myself and them to meet certain benchmarks. I see our purpose differently: We are here to embrace the human experience. Our bodies serve as vessels, allowing us to feel, taste, and perceive the world. Thus, our primary aim becomes exploration, indulging in our chosen experiences. This could range from becoming an exemplary leader to a spiritually attuned one.

Consequently, leading an organization is less about pushing for tangible achievements and more about facilitating a collective journey of discovery. Whether the team aims to double the turnover or introduce a novel healthcare system, it's about the experience of pursuing that ambition rather than just the end goal itself. Ultimately, the journey and its learnings take precedence over the destination; the specifics are simply a matter of choice.

At the age of 27, I started questioning life. I got into leadership roles and had long, heavy working days full of meetings with people who did not listen to or connect with each other. They were too occupied expressing their own opinion, arguing, and being political rather than explore issues and ascend to greater knowing. I had come to find my days more and more meaningless. Simultaneously, I was getting married, and we were discussing the idea of building a family. We had lots of hopes and dreams for the future. The long working hours made me think, "Is this what life is supposed to be? Work your ass off for money or for people far away that don't even know you exist or care about how you feel or who you are?" Getting this experience early in my career revealed that everything is about people; everything else is "technology" somehow. It gave me deep insight, but at the same time, it almost made me quit before my career even started.

As an intuitive, empath, and highly sensory individual, I let this situation drain my energy. And I started to get depressed.

I thought, "There has got to be something more!"

From an early age, the voice inside whispered and wanted to be heard. The spirit called. I started to dive deep into everything that could open the door to the great mystery while trying to continue my career as a leader, become a father, and make a good life for my family. Yet, the duality and struggle to follow my newly discovered path and still feed the old path had turned my incredibly life complex.

As often happens, the universe presents a powerful message at the right moment. I found an article about a man whose experience deeply resonated with me. Much like my own journey, he had undergone an awakening and contemplated leaving the corporate world to become a spiritual teacher. I, too, had been drawn to teaching yoga and meditation.

Upon discussing his thoughts with mentors, he received some enlightening advice: "Not everyone is supposed to be spiritual gurus; some are here to share their gifts in the business world." This perspective led him to an epiphany. He realized he didn't have to choose — he could be spiritually attuned and thrive in the corporate world. Embracing this dual path, he became the first sustainability director of a global corporation. Today, he stands as an accomplished investor.

His story inspired me. It solidified my decision to persist in the business domain, and I became eager to explore and master the essence of true leadership.

It was a challenging choice, and it has been quite a journey.

The life we choose gives us plenty of awakening opportunities; life is a playground, and we decide as spirits to explore this through a human experience. So, for example, at some awareness level, we may explore what it would be like to be a leader, just as someone else decides to be an artist.

When we make choices and start to live by them, reality will send situations with possibilities and challenges that we need, in some way, to benefit from or learn from, to mature, to realize, and to get insights into something new. Our ability to navigate this beautiful chaos inside and out is what unfolds our potential; that's our self-leadership. Self-leadership decides if we will be leaders if others make us their leaders.

The artist might face challenges, such as nobody buying his art, so he has to compensate with other work to do what he wants. There is also the fear of performance, procrastination, or struggling to make that first exhibition happen—struggling with self-esteem and worthiness. Then, he must walk through these obstacles blocking his path in order to emerge in his new, more prosperous version on the other side.

The spirit-full leader might face challenges like being misunderstood, considered weak or soft, or too concerned about others, humanity, climate change, or welfare. She might also meet many people who like and trust her but do not take her intuitive skills seriously. And maybe she is such a visionary, far into unknown territory, that she does not know how to explain herself. Yet, on the other hand, she knows and is completely intuitive without any traditional structure.

All this is only a portal to increased awareness and higher consciousness. To awakening.

The key to a spirit-full of self-leadership is to learn to see all our challenges as opportunities to grow and meet them with an open heart (and mind). The key is to increase our awareness of what part of ourselves, our authentic personas or our survival strategies, controls, blocks, or enhances our self-leadership.

Our self-leadership, the way we make choices, behave like human beings, and lead ourselves about everything and everyone, reveals which agenda or underlying programming we execute. What energy or frequency level is our operating system running at? It will define the acts we manifest ourselves.

Everyday Spirit-Full Leadership

When thinking of how spirit-fullness shows up in leadership, the first thing that springs to my mind is the compassion and generosity that love can manifest. We care for, or start to care for, the greater good and assent to life, nature, and everything living. We show respect for our opponent, maybe even empathy or compassion. We do not try to kill him with our arguments. We first listen, and we first try to understand his viewpoint. Where did he come from? And, of course, we never attack. We do not see someone else as a competitor. We see them as someone who has chosen the same thing we have done.

Maybe we can learn from their success. Perhaps we can copy or even co-create with them. We are no longer only in it for the gain. We are in it for the experience, and the effect of that might be a good result. In my experience and many others, getting to our target state takes more energy when we fight to get something. When we relax and play with the background, like a sport or a business, we usually reach our goals more easily and sustainably. Fighting for something will never be sustainable, and we will only have to continue to fight.

I try to act out of honest intention, as we are in this life together. We are in the same boat. I am not trying to be clever and manipulate the other party. I maintain a straightforward, honest approach. I have treated my vendors transparently and negotiated openly in a win-win strategy. That has benefited my experience in every way. My competitors, I have treated as friends and my managers, colleagues, and subordinates as family. Treat your peers as you want to be treated yourself. Often, when I have left a role, my vendors have shown more appreciation than my employer. They have appreciated being seen, heard, and treated as partners in a way they have never been used to.

We are not always in balance. A situation I've experienced shows how it can be when people are under extraordinary pressure in an ordinary work life. I was in a position where I was under pressure both at work and in life in general, and that resulted in severe exhaustion. I had felt fatigued for quite a while when I summoned the courage to speak to my CEO and said I was not feeling well and had difficulty coping with the situation. I was messed up.

I simultaneously had two executive assignments as R&D director and HR director, and life at home was not easy. It was a pretty stupid choice by me, but that was how I was then, invincible. I did not feel well, I wanted to reduce my workload to care for myself and my home situation. I seriously thought about quitting my job but did not want to do that. I somehow liked it.

I've never felt more vulnerable in my life. Stepping in and saying that I couldn't do it was not part of my vocabulary back then. My CEO replied that life could be a struggle, and he explained that he himself looked in the mirror every morning, telling himself that he was strong. He told me to increase my speed during the last period of my second assignment, and that everything would be okay if I cheered up a little.

That might have been true, but that did not work for me at the time. I was already too drained of energy, and my body had started shutting down. It is the process in which the body tries to reach the inhabitant to tell them, "Hey you, you need to stop right now, or we have to try to get your attention more dramatically, like giving you a real smack on the head or an illness of some kind to make you slow down."

Two days later, I called the company's healthcare. I got therapy and kept myself together with the help of all my mindfulness tricks.

I clung to the hope of recovery for six strenuous months, but therapy seemed futile. The root cause of my situation remained unchanged, and I found myself bereft of the strength to alter it. I felt that the only recourse was to surrender completely. My physician could see the toll it took on me and prescribed a rest period. Drained, I took a hiatus from the office that lasted five long months. During this time, I wrestled with doubt and, at one point, genuinely believed I might never return. My defeat bore heavily on me, leading me to contemplate the unthinkable.

However, amidst the engulfing darkness, a flicker of life force reignited deep within me, manifesting in an unfamiliar yet potent manner. With newfound determination, I rose again. Not only did I return to complete my assignments, but I also emerged with profound gratitude for the challenges I'd set upon myself and the unwavering support I've received during this tumultuous phase.

I don't blame my CEO. He was under tremendous pressure and is a great guy. That's what stress can do to a person, both him and me. I know he meant well, which was how he had coped with the pressure. What I needed in that situation was a little more empathy, not pity, but genuine compassion.

Many leaders, including myself, often equate leadership with toughness and being strong. However, I've realized that true strength lies in gentleness and empathy. During a challenging period in my life, I understood the essence of real strength. Ironically, I had to experience a loss of my perceived strength to discover its true nature.

Spirit-full leaders know how to connect with spirit in a situation. They know or learn that the problem is a wake-up call, a call to awaken to a new level.

I believe this is why we see a big difference in world leaders. The ones we look up to and respect are balanced and empathic. They are self-contained, not self-absorbed. They don't try to be something; they just are.

Another episode took place early in my career. Some years ago, I read the article I had previously mentioned. I described this situation in our book *A Journey of Riches—The Way of the Leader*, but it also applies here.

I was in my office when I overheard a conversation, or, I would say, one person yelling at another in the office on the other side of the hall. They were arguing about late deliveries within the project we all worked on. I could hear that the guy being yelled at felt very bad about the situation and that the guy who was yelling was upset and frustrated. That was something the situation in the project at the time could make us all feel. The argument continued for a while and ended when the guy being yelled at gave up and said, "Okay, okay," with a dejected voice. The yeller turned around and walked away without a word.

After a while, I went over to my colleague (the guy who was yelled at) and asked how he was. He looked at me with hopelessness and said, "I'm okay. I can't manage my workload right now; it's too much, and the pile is getting bigger." I stood there in silence; he did not want to talk anymore, and I felt strongly that I should not say anything else. Finally, I said, "I'll be in my office if you want to talk."

I went back to my office and continued with my work. My colleague came over ten minutes later and sat at my desk. He said, "I just want to say how much I appreciated you coming over to ask how I was." He continued, "Actually, it's you who would have the biggest reason to yell at me because it's to you I owe my deliveries first, and in our project, we have our biggest delay, and you don't yell. Instead, you ask how I am and if you can do something for me, and you do that often." He added, "I will make sure to catch up."

Which he did! I was pretty stunned by the feedback. It came directly from the heart and touched mine. I felt a warmth inside, and I could say how much I appreciated him. It was a moment where souls met in silent understanding.

My small act of compassion was acknowledging his humanness and vulnerability. I stood by him. I gave space. He could be just what he was at that moment, and it seemed like it helped him find his spirit again, and then he knew how to prioritize. He knew what to do. This situation happened early in my career and taught me something about spirit-full leadership. There and then, it made me understand compassion and empathy. I figured out later that the deeper energy I had felt at that moment was gratitude, which has a significant role in being a leader.

As managers, we usually spend our time parked in our mind box, focusing on the outside, trying to figure out the next step, the result, or the strategy. We get lost in performing today's tasks because we believe we have to. We blindly perform and meet neither ourselves nor the other in how it feels to experience being human in that moment. If we spent just a minute tuning in deeper with ourselves and the others before acting, our leadership would be much more empowering. As an effect, we would perform our work more efficiently, and it would be more fun because we would feel more appreciated.

Spirit-full leadership means being a high-frequency fellow human being—someone who embodies love, compassion, joy, and peace and is concerned with the well-being of others and the environment.

"The leadership spirit comes with a spirit of leadership."

~ Myles Munroe

The Essence of Spirit-full Leadership

————————∞◯⌀◯∞————————

E veryone has the power to change the world. As humans, we vastly underestimate the power we wield, and there isn't one person on the planet who doesn't want to incite even a slight change in their corner of the world. The desire to change and evolve is innate within all of us at some level. Change starts with leadership because as much as we naturally desire to grow, we fear the unknown. As my co-author, Stefan poetically pointed out, "Spirit-full leadership is our natural alignment with love."

A parent desires their home to be a certain way. A boss wants his organization to be orderly and embody their vision. A teacher wishes their classes to be interactive with their students attentive. Now, think of the above roles you have experienced. Think about situations where love permeated the atmosphere in these environments. Think of the home you walk into and as a result, begin to feel relaxed, at ease, and willing to open yourself up to chat or listen. Have you ever had a boss who was more like a friend, and made it easier for you to be responsible for your duties? What about the teacher who smiles and sings in class to bring the best out in you? These are examples of people who desire to make a difference in the lives of the people in their care by breathing fresh air into their spirits.

It feels good to be in the presence of a leader who embraces the spirit of love in their leadership style. They have an insatiable drive, an unmatched desire to make a difference, and a vision that transcends the typical way of doing things. Think about the household you have walked into and felt uncomfortable in but couldn't figure out why. I'm sure you had a boss who ruled with an iron fist, making you feel like an easily replaceable number. And who hasn't had a teacher you felt should be running Hell rather than a classroom? Are you starting to understand the distinct difference between the two opposite sides of the coin?

Both are part of the same coin because sometimes we must experience walking on eggshells, the inconsiderate dictator boss, and the strict teacher stifling creativity. Didn't all the great leaders of history go through some form of adversity on the road to awakening to the essence of their truth? From the invisible energy that Gandhi used to free his people from slave labor to Mandela uniting a country, both leaders faced seemingly insurmountable challenges. They had a deep connection with the essence of who they were. Call it spirit, call it a connection to their higher self, or call it faith. Whatever you want to name it, they had an undeniable presence that drew people towards them.

The question is, how did they become that way? Stefan and I intend to share this information throughout this book, and we invite you to dive deep with us.

Asleep to your Abilities

Many motivational speakers and leadership authors believe leaders are created rather than born. I would argue the opposite. We are all born leaders and have instead been deprogrammed while growing up. We were natural leaders as children, curious and humble, hungry for knowledge to fuel our incredibly vivid imaginations.

When we knew exactly what we wanted, we were persistent and determined to get it, and we could motivate, inspire, and influence everyone around us to help achieve our objective. We are born in spirit, and life disconnects us from the source of our creation. So what went wrong?

We became accustomed to hearing "No," "Don't," and "Can't" as children. "That's wrong! Stop that!" Most of our parents advised us to be quiet and not to bother the grownups with "stupid" questions. Many teachers continued to tell us what we could and couldn't do in high school and what was possible. Unfortunately, traditional education does not prepare students to be leaders. Instead, it prepares them to take orders and follow the rules. Instead of learning to be creative, independent, and self-sufficient thinkers, many know to comply and rationally follow regulations to keep the corporate machine running.

To develop the leader within you and live your fullest life, I feel the first step is to unlearn by recognizing and honoring yourself. To regain your effectiveness as a spirit-full leader, you must be daring, open the door to your inner kingdom, where your childhood fantasies reside, and journey to the heart.

The most crucial characteristic for spirit-full leaders to cultivate is self-awareness. Can you see things from many different perspectives? Can you hold two opposite viewpoints to be accurate, accepting them simultaneously?

Korn/Ferry International, the global consulting firm, discovered in a study of 486 publicly traded companies that organizations with great financial success have employees with higher degrees of self-awareness than companies with poor economic performance.

Self-awareness, however, appears to be in scarce supply among leaders. While women in executive-level management positions are more self-aware than men in similar situations, the aggregate percentages indicate that there is still room for improvement. The Hay Group Research found that 19% of women executives interviewed exhibited self-awareness, compared to 4% of their male colleagues in a sample of 17,000 people tested globally.

In spirit-full leadership, where passion, inspiration, and positive energy drive a team toward greatness, a foundational trait is paramount in its influence: self-awareness. At the core of this vibrant leadership style lies the leader's ability to recognize and understand their emotions, strengths, weaknesses, values, and motivations. Self-awareness is the shining light that illuminates the path to authentic and impactful leadership, empowering the leader to create an environment of trust, empathy, and collaboration.

Knowing yourself is essential because you are the only constant factor in your pursuits. I have found meditation to be one of the best ways to go within for answers and keep the connection to self. I attended a meditation center called Heartfulness Meditation while visiting a friend at the end of 2013 in Chennai, India. My friend Rajeesh had invited me over after our work together for a personal development company based in Ubud, Bali, where I was running the sales team. The meditation practiced was called Heart Yoga. Three times a day, we would sit in chairs in a huge outdoor hall with men on one side and women on the other.

The guru, or one of his disciples, would sit in a chair at the front of the room connected with his heart, opening the divine through the previous guru who had transitioned and sending loving energy to the hearts of hundreds of people sitting in front of them. The sessions lasted for an hour. I mostly felt centered and in a heightened consciousness, feeling completely present and connected to everything. At other times, anger hurt, and frustration arose, disappearing once I fully felt the emotion, expanding my level of awareness. I also had two sit-downs with the guru's disciples.

The process is simple: you both sit in a chair opposite each other, close your eyes, and the disciple channels divine energy through the guru, removing any energy blocks that you might have and simultaneously empowering your chakras. According to Dr. Travis Bradberry, author of *Emotional Intelligence 2.0*, self-awareness is a critical component of emotional intelligence. He describes emotional intelligence as "the ability to identify and understand emotions in yourself and others as well as the ability to control your actions and relationships using this understanding."

Self-awareness is liberating because you deepen the connection with yourself. This allows you to make better decisions—to change or grow and to see things from many different perspectives. It's the keystone to the arc of spirit-full leadership, infusing authenticity, emotional intelligence, empathy, personal growth, and resilience into the leader's approach. With a deep understanding of themselves, spirit-full leaders create an environment where trust thrives, innovation flourishes, and each team member is empowered to unleash their full potential. As the spirit-full leader finds their true essence through self-awareness, it ignites a powerful spark that illuminates the path to greatness.

Within the journey of spirit-full leadership, the leader's willingness to embrace personal growth is vital. Self-awareness acts as a mirror, reflecting areas for improvement and revealing paths to development. This humility and commitment to continuous change elevates the leader's capabilities and inspires team members to embark on their own journeys of self-improvement, creating a culture of excellence and ambition.

Although I no longer practice Heart Yoga meditation in the traditional way it was taught, I have a morning routine that is non-negotiable for me. I haven't missed a day in over 1,500 days, and I track this through the Insight Timer app. I feel this level of discipline is necessary for forever awareness and personal growth. Expanding into our limitless potential is one of the gifts of life, and there is always another level. When you stand at the peak and wake up to your abilities, you receive another challenge highlighting several higher elevations for you to climb. I was lucky enough to learn that I was harboring dormant potential, resources left untapped, and could have easily conformed to living a mundane life without a sense of curiosity.

Although I feel like I'm constantly awakening, I had a series of defining moments that changed my life forever. One such moment was Australia Day, January 26th, 2010, in Bondi Beach, in the Eastern suburbs of Sydney. I was celebrating with a handful of mates, and after doing a line of cocaine in the bathrooms, washing the residue of powder up my nose, I caught a glimpse of myself in the mirror. I felt a sense of disgust; I realized that I despised myself. In that instant, I could feel self-loathing's hold over me. It was like that. I couldn't get enough of what I despised and hated myself. Retraining myself from smashing the mirror, I looked deeper into my eyes with a well of sadness, and I knew that I needed to make changes in my life.

I decided never to touch recreational drugs again, and I was already meditating at home on and off. I knew I needed a lifestyle change; I eased up on my intake of alcohol, substituting beer with ginger beer and then tea. I joined a meditation group, making new friends, and I joined a year-long coaching program designed to transform your life and clients' lives. In addition to the program, I attended weekly workshops and seminars to saturate myself in positivity and completely overhaul my mindset. Later that year, I sold my landscape business and became a full-time coach. However, to people outside, it appeared that I had made rapid changes in less than 12 months. The reality is that after some self-reflection, I learned that I had been leaning toward this lifestyle for some time; I just wasn't fully aware of it.

I've discovered that through consistent effort, you can transform what your life reflects by what you habitually decide to do each day. Every day is an opportunity to awaken to a deeper version of ourselves, and having a morning routine is one of the ways I have found to maintain that level of curiosity for expansion in all areas of my life. Below are four techniques to help you become more self-aware.

1. Develop a Meditation Practice

Meditation has existed for thousands of years and is a common practice. As you've read, meditation has played a massive part in both Stefan's and my lives. Now, science has finally proven what the mystics, sages, and Taoists have known all along: that even short periods of meditation calm the mind, allowing the meditator to access heightened states of awareness.

Scientists worldwide have measured the brain wave frequency of meditators for years, and it's common knowledge that theta brain wave activity occurring in deep sleep or meditation sharpens self-awareness and raises consciousness. There are many different types of meditation, and I found it best to close your eyes and sit still for twenty minutes. Preferably seated in a chair or on the floor, close your eyes and allow any thoughts to come and go while you focus on your breath. It is that easy and that difficult.

Meditation is a transformative practice for spirit-full leaders seeking to deepen their self-awareness. Leaders can navigate challenges with greater wisdom, authenticity, and compassion by nurturing a heightened sense of introspection, emotional intelligence, and resilience. As a result, they can foster a positive and energizing work environment or align a family with an inspiring and empowering goal with less arguing. Like brushing your teeth or taking a shower, meditation works best when you practice every day, even if it's for only five minutes.

2. Take Self-Awareness Tests

Taking tests to measure self-awareness is a great way to gauge where you are personally and professionally. I have found the following tests quite helpful: the Insight Quiz, The LoGreco Self-Awareness Quiz, the iNLP Center Self-Awareness Test, and the How Self-Aware Are You? Quiz, and the Self-Awareness Test.

These tests assess your personality, behavior, and leadership style. Engaging in such assessments can provide valuable feedback and self-reflection opportunities, uncovering blind spots that reveal your leadership style, validate your strengths, and empower you to use them effectively to motivate and inspire others.

For the last seven years, I have been using Insightimer to track and measure how often I meditate, do breath work, affirmations, read, exercise, do chakra meditation, self-reiki and whether I practice yoga daily. Doing at least one of the above has been a non-negotiable, and I'm disciplined with it as it sets up the rest of my day and brings me an abundance of inner peace. I haven't missed a day in over 1500 days or over three years.

3. External Factors Should Be Recognized

Through meditation, it becomes easier to determine what variables, triggers, or positive and negative indicators cause others to act in a certain way toward you. What motivates you to do what you do, and how do others react to your actions? In turn, how do you react, and why do you react the way you do? What effect does culture have on your perceptions and those of others? The answers to these questions will help you understand yourself more deeply. The following are three sub-categories for you to ponder.

i) Collect Reliable Feedback

Feedback fosters empathy and allows you to see how your actions affect others. Being oblivious of personal blind spots—traits or features that may limit how you act, respond, conduct, or believe, and hence limit your effectiveness—is one of the primary signs of low self-awareness or being overworked and stressed.

Consider undergoing a 360-degree assessment involving feedback from multiple sources, including subordinates, peers, superiors, and even yourself. This comprehensive evaluation provides a well-rounded view of your leadership strengths and areas needing improvement.

ii) Consider the Circumstances

Consider when you should use a character trait to your favor and when you should ignore it. The most self-aware, spirit-full leaders understand their biases and adapt their behavior to reshape their public image. Rather than undergoing a complete personality overhaul, they hone their authenticity with finesse. They meticulously assess situations that demand specific personality traits, discerning when characteristics like extraversion or openness are pivotal and when they are not.

iii) Examine Actions In The Context Of Your Priorities And Values

Do you notice any trends in your actions? Examine those patterns regarding what matters to you, what motivates you, and who you want to be. When weighing competing priorities, be honest with yourself. Do you have any habits that you'd like to change? Are there any other variables you'd want to consider? Finding out what makes you amazing and doing more of it is the best result of self-awareness. Continue to add to, polish, and expand that list. On the other hand, try to be less aware of what has a negative impact on you, others, and your intended objectives.

4. Regular Self-Reflection

Our tendencies are influenced by our culture, backgrounds, and experiences, yet we are ultimately in charge of who we become. New situations can also lead to different reactions or triggers. Keep an open mind, and don't stop tapping into and uncovering the essence of your spirit. Set aside dedicated time for self-reflection regularly.

During this time, contemplate your thoughts, emotions, actions, and experiences. Consider what went well, what challenges you faced, and how you responded to them. Ask yourself probing questions about your values, motivations, and aspirations as a leader.

Journaling can be an effective tool during self-reflection, allowing you to capture your thoughts and gain deeper insights into your inner world. It's a profound tool for self-awareness, enabling spirit-full leaders to delve into their thoughts, emotions, and experiences. By making journaling a regular practice, you can refine their self-awareness, strengthen their leadership approach, and create a more positive and inspiring impact on their team, organization, and even dynamics within their friendships and family.

In the realm of spirit-full leadership, where passion, purpose, and positive energy converge to inspire greatness, there exists a profound truth: self-awareness is the beacon that guides the way. A spirit-full leader who embarks on the journey of self-awareness gains a deep understanding of their thoughts, emotions, values, and actions. This awareness becomes the foundation for authentic, empathetic, and impactful personal development.

"The Growth and development of people is the highest calling of leadership."

~ Harvey Firestone

Self-Awareness is a Lifestyle

Through the practice of self-awareness, spirit-full leaders cultivate a deep connection with their true selves. This authenticity is a powerful magnet, drawing their team members closer and fostering an environment of trust and respect. By understanding their strengths and weaknesses, they can leverage their unique talents to ignite the spark of inspiration in those they lead.

Emotional intelligence flourishes within the heart of self-aware leaders. This heightened emotional awareness allows them to navigate the ebb and flow of emotions gracefully, fostering an atmosphere of empathy and compassion. They lead not only with their minds but also with their hearts, forging genuine connections that inspire loyalty and dedication.

Self-awareness provides spirit-full leaders with a roadmap to resilience. In the face of challenges, they stand unwavering, having discovered the wellsprings of their inner strength. Armed with this fortitude, they guide anything within their influence through adversity, demonstrating that setbacks are but stepping stones on the path to success.

Spirit-full leaders align their actions with their values and purpose by delving into the depths of self-awareness. This congruence creates a harmonious leadership style that resonates with the team's collective aspirations. They lead not for personal gain but for the greater good, united by a shared vision of improving the world.

The importance of self-awareness to spirit-full leadership cannot be overstated. The compass guides leaders toward their true selves, empowering them to inspire, uplift, and empower those they lead. Embracing self-awareness is the key that unlocks the door to a profound and purposeful leadership journey, leaving an indelible mark on the hearts and minds of all who walk alongside them. As spirit-full leaders cultivate self-awareness, they illuminate the path to unlimited potential, forging a legacy that transcends time and inspires future generations.

Tapping into our spirit and releasing past conditioning is a transformative process that empowers us to become spirit-full leaders in our community, career, and family. It begins with a journey of self-discovery, where we delve into the depths of our inner selves and connect with our true essence. We unveil our passions, values, and purpose by seeking stillness and introspection, laying the foundation for authentic leadership.

Awakening your talents and releasing past conditioning is pivotal to becoming a spirit-full leader. Our past experiences and societal influences often shape our beliefs and behaviors, creating unconscious patterns that limit our potential. We liberate ourselves from their constraints by acknowledging and understanding these conditioning factors. We unlock the door to personal growth and empowerment as we heal past wounds and let go of limiting beliefs.

As spirit-full leaders, we embrace vulnerability as a strength rather than a weakness. Being open and authentic about our experiences and challenges creates a safe and supportive environment for others to do the same. Our vulnerability fosters trust and connection, allowing us to form meaningful relationships with our community, colleagues, and family members. In this environment of trust, we can lead with empathy and compassion, understanding the feelings and needs of those we serve and responding with genuine care and understanding.

One of the routines we did at the personal development company that I mentioned at the beginning of this chapter was a circle of trust every morning. It entailed reciting the Prayer of Saint Francis and answering five questions.

1. What are you most grateful for today?

2. What is challenging us the most?

3. What is one thing we did well?

4. What is one thing we could improve?

5. Are we clear of conflict with everyone within the company?

We all sat in a circle, holding space and listening to each person's words. We all agreed that our team meetings would be judgment-free spaces with no advice-giving or problem-solving. It was a space for complete freedom of expression to voice whatever was on your mind and heart. I found it empowering to be heard and speak my truth and I know everyone I was close with felt the same. There were a couple of heated moments you would expect when you work and live together, but everything was resolved through listening without interruption. There were many heartfelt, vulnerable shares, too. We learned a lot about each other's strengths and weaknesses and how best to support one another. We bonded as a team, increasing our respect and trust for each other.

I learned that we empower others by nurturing their strengths and talents and fostering a culture of support in our community, career, and family. Ultimately, tapping into our spirit and releasing past conditioning can embody the true essence of spirit-full leadership in every aspect of our lives.

"Spiritual leadership is the power to change the atmosphere by one's presence, the unconscious influence that makes Christ and spiritual things real to others."

~ J Oswald Sanders

Exercising Awakening

⌒◦⟋⟍◦⌒

C an we train ourselves to awaken and embrace spirit-full leadership?

Unfortunately, the answer is no, but we can ask for it, wish for it, and be allowed to wake up to it. Awakening only happens by letting go of what we believed in; all our illusions and delusions, and everything we thought was right about our perception of reality. Still, even if it's about letting go, awakening is like a muscle that needs training and unknown territory.

Just as when going to the gym, the weight we work out with is neither resistance nor what we encounter in life. Weight is a support for getting the correct tension to the muscle. What supports our awakening are the challenges of life itself.

Why do so many of us search for and seek awakening or enlightenment? Probably because over the years, we have cut ourselves off from our genuine connection to nature and our spirit. And we awaken to the fact that there has got to be something more. But, unfortunately, because of our schooling—our "well-educated minds" as John Spender, my fellow author, describes it—we think that enlightenment is something we must find, something we have to invent by thinking, often outside ourselves. And it's true; enlightenment is outside as well as inside.

Roberto Assagioli, the father of integrative psychosynthesis theory, explained man as a complex but at the same time rational "system." Our self is a center of pure consciousness connected to our superconscious. Assagioli holistically took on all perspectives of humanness, spirit, soul, body, psyche, and environment. He explained that we hide from ourselves by being unconscious of most parts of what controls us, our programming and patterns enclosed in our persona. Exploring how we mirror ourselves in the world can help us uncover our habits and become more conscious of our underlying programming and superconscious potential, as explained in Buddhism, Zen, Taoism, Energy medicine, and other philosophies.

Assagioli's theories explained the free spirit as having a human experience in a simple Western way. The journey I've embarked on has been a challenging discovery of Assagioli's teachings. I would have probably never understood what he truly described if I had not gained the experience of being a free spirit in a body before studying his theories.

We can always wonder where the initial spark comes from to awaken. It's not necessary to explain it. We can try to make complex explanations and systems of awakening or the spark itself. It will not change anything, and the sensation we experience will exist just as much anyway. So, we can give thanks when awakening comes and let it give us more clarity. There is no need or use to protest; it's impossible to turn back anyway, under any circumstance, and why would we want to continue living in the fog? No. There is only one moment, and it's now. There is only one direction, and it's forward.

The muscle that needs to be trained is also a result of that spark. Though it's not powered by willpower, the muscle is prepared by letting everything be as it is while exploring what is. So be the Zen

Master, curious about this human experience without hurting any living thing or leaving a trace behind.

There are no definite answers, and the mystery is too vast. The spirit-full leader knows this, and she has peace knowing that there is nothing to achieve and nothing to understand, just an exploration of living the adventure full of life. That's when the connection opens. She knows that spirit-full leadership is a willingness to listen and follow, make herself available, and serve. There is no use in conquering, commanding, or supervising. Instead, she gives energy and direction based on love, embracing all flaws and misconceptions to leave them behind. The power of love wants to be experienced in every one of us, simple as that.

It's said that God hid the Holy Grail in the last place man would look. So, it was hidden in our hearts. We can wonder why he did that, but I guess it's because that's the connection point, or very close, where spirit meets the body and, as such, earth.

And maybe that's why we often say that great leaders, great spirit-full leaders, have big, brave, vulnerable hearts.

The great children's book author Astrid Lindgren, the creator of the character Pippi Långstrump (Pippi Longstocking, the world's strongest girl), said, "What would happen if there was a war, and no one went to it." In my interpretation, she means that if no one acts regarding a conflict, there will be no conflict. She means we have a responsibility to not follow someone else's decision but rather make our own. That quote is from a true spirit-full leader who has inspired many generations worldwide with her stories.

"**True leadership is about connecting with the deeper spiritual essence within ourselves and others, guiding our organizations towards a purpose that transcends profit alone.**"

~ Alper Tanca

Universal Truth

S pirit-full leaders know to find their way by acting on universal truths, not made-up ones.

Throughout history, men have invented truths that have become religions because they serve their purpose and can benefit them.

We have created the business religion, the science-religion, the politics religion, the Darwinism religion, the sports religion, the culture religion, the religion of religions, and so on.

The hardcore business world runs according to the business religion: everything that is right for the business, for the market, is a truth, and we praise the holy money. It's a religion, and we are stuck in that drama. To hardcore scientists, nothing is the truth unless it can be scientifically proven with statistics and evidence. Stuck in the science-religion, they can't see that there was something before we started with science. For those stuck in politics, politics has turned into a religion. They obey the political code and are stuck in debate, blame games, and the fight for power. And the religion of religions is the same. Being Catholic, Buddhist, Protestant, or Muslim only means that we have obeyed and put our truth into a made-up perspective of reality.

"Love is not a product of reasoning and statistics.
It just comes—none knows whence— and cannot explain
itself. Love is madness; if thwarted, it develops fast.
When you fish for love, bait with your heart,
not your brain."
—Mark Twain

There is nothing wrong with living according to a "religion." Most people do that, in some way or another. The truth is that religion is not true, and it is that religion is not true and gives us a limited form of seeing and experiencing reality.

These religions are only true if we maintain at a certain level of consciousness. Spirit-full leaders awaken and appear within every context but ascend beyond these religions.

We humans spend a lot of energy trying to convince others that "our religion is the truth," and we look down on others who do not live by our religion. Sometimes, we mix these ideas so much that we get tangled in deep drama. We even start wars to prove our point, even in our time, in the so-called enlightened world. That's how sophisticated we have become.

Sometimes, we say that these religions have nothing to do with each other. Or do they? For instance, we reason that sports and politics have nothing to do with each other. We justify having a sports event like the Olympics in a country that is at war with another country or in a country that violates basic human rights. That's an example of a dramatic mix of religions, business, politics, and sports that could start fires or unite at best.

As soon as we rise above these made-up truths called religions, we can see that all these are only made up because we need some structure, a belief, or truth to hold on to. We need to claim power or rationalize reality so that it serves our purpose.

This is reasonable because pure emptiness can make a man completely mad if they do not understand the authentic experience.

We constantly invent new truths because we need something to hold on to, to fill the void.

Viktor Frankl gives a hardcore view of this in his book *Man's Search for Meaning*, where he tells the story of his survival at Auschwitz concentration camp during WWII. Yet even under devastating circumstances, he gave his life meaning and purpose, which no one could take away. They could have even taken his life but never his soul. And so, he did not only survive, but he also invented a theory about the human psyche, which he wrote down on tiny pieces of paper during that time.

What is a universal truth? The law of attraction (like attracts like) or Albert Einstein's relativity theory, $E=mc^2$, are known universal truths or close to at least. A universal truth is a condition beyond the human mind's influence. We can, for instance, see that energy flows around, manifesting itself in its way without our interference unless we give it a direction. Then, we choose to do something with it.

The energy might manifest as a tree, a river, food, a fish, or a human being. If we human beings, for instance, invest energy in aggression, we will attract people who want to fight, discuss, debate, or make duality. And we humans love a good fight, and the more we love it, the more we attract it. Humankind has chosen battle so much that we have filled our reality with it. Every sports event has it, the stock market has it, every boardroom has it, politics has it, and we love it. We have forgotten that even the playful combat, like in sports actually attracts fights in many other forms that we do not like.

As Assagioli described, humanity filters energy through its underlying programming in many ways. By doing that, we create the reality we live in.

Spirit-full leaders know how to see through the distortions and attract greatness. First, they see greatness in others by being great themselves. Then, by being humane and working together, they amplify and multiply their direct energy to expand it. That's a universal truth that comes to life.

Perseverance

Picture a big tree and a blade of grass. Both have perseverance, and both have resilience. The tree stands tall, naturally, and so does the blade of grass. The tree knows it's a tree. An oak does not compete with a pine. An apple tree does not think it should grow pears. The blade of grass does not compete with the other blades of grass. It just stands there and grows and expands because it can, because that's what it does, for no particular reason.

The tree and the blade of grass both have their roots spread out and buried deep into the soil. They are connected with other trees and blades of grass. They are related and aligned. They are the source, a unique representation of the life force.

Heavy winds can break them, or the dry season could stress them out, or storms, tornados, and severe fires may destroy them. But for the most part, they stand tall and waggle with the wind, still standing proud.

Mother Nature is the greatest healer, and she is ever-present. This has been proven repeatedly. She changes, transforms, and lives on with more perseverance than before. So many human civilizations have risen and fallen, and when they're abandoned, Mother Nature recovers and transforms the land. Where there have been buildings, nature grows forests again, enveloping the structures. An example is Chernobyl, the nuclear power plant in Ukraine that exploded in the early 1980s. It's very unhealthy for people to be there, but nature has grown back and taken over the nearby city that was evacuated. Nature does this all when the land is left without human interference.

Take climate change as another example. Mother Nature does not negotiate about her health; she shows what change she goes through and how she deals with her circumstances. She will continue living, but the circumstances for humankind might not be so good anymore. We humans can negotiate our way of living and sharing this planet. We do not control this planet, even if we seem to think so. We have been allowed to live here. Could we make it a win-win—a win for you, me, and Mother Earth, united?

Mother Nature is the ultimate guide and shows us the perseverance and resilience of a spirit-full leader. And maybe that's why many spirit-full leaders express a solid connection to nature, describing how they seek solitude and rejuvenation.

A person strongly connected to nature often shows great concern for others, is empathic and humble, and knows that we are only an insignificant parenthesis in Earth's history. A spirit-full leader understands that we, in our insignificance, have the abundance of living with and by nature.

The Healer

The spirit-full leader is a strong and true healer. Healing means to put together, to make what's been separated whole, aligned, or united. And the spirit-full leaders join, bringing harmony to the situation, which history has proven.

When awakening happens, we also start to be aware of our own healing abilities, though many spirit-full leaders are unaware that that is what they do. They heal the circumstance, the organization, and the business just by their presence, being, and actions. Their maturity, inner security, clarity, common sense, heartfulness, and authenticity sweep through like the wind, bringing higher frequencies to the situation.

They bring their light to the situation—a new light, perspective, and skill. They stand for valid human values and unite an organization by listening and cultivating a democratic and peaceful approach to things and people.

Some stand on the barricades proclaiming civil rights and the necessity of climate change; some make inventions that clean the ocean; some are school teachers; and some are musicians, artists, or even spiritual teachers.

History has given us several spirit-full leaders to know and by whose example we can be inspired. I think of people like Mahatma Gandhi, Nelson Mandela, Martin Luther King, Jr, Eleanor Roosevelt, Dag Hammarskjöld, Bono, Barack Obama, Lao Tzu, and many more. People who do their utmost to create thriving circumstances give the cause a voice, report injustice, negotiate, or unite the world into peace by administrative and diplomatic means.

These people are more on the scene as politicians, artists, or spiritual persons. Examples from the business world are not that easy to spot. They often keep a low profile and are out of the news.

None of the above call themselves healers (that we know of). They do not claim the skills to heal or call themselves spiritual leaders or spirit-full leaders, but that's the fundamentals of the character of the spirit-full leader.

The fundamental of healing is to have an honest, heart-centered intention. A true healer does not want anything from the person or circumstance that is to be healed. Likewise, the healer does not need anything from the other.

Spirit-full leaders act with honest intentions, are heart-centered, and are dedicated to a do-good cause. They work with a love-based agenda, not a result-based one. Their thinking, actions, and operations are based on solid human values like equal rights and solidarity. They probably have a voice that says, "This can't be right. It has to be something more."

When we awaken and rise above the drama within the "religions" that define us, we will be more aware of what has controlled us. We will be free to act out of honest intention with great integrity within the religion. It will not matter what others do or do not do; we, as spirit-full leaders, will know our way and act by inner navigation.

When we awaken, we start to experience and become aware of our feminine and masculine aspects. They will tune in and get in balance so that the drama between man and woman disappears and the attraction matures. The drama is only there as long as we are stuck in the fog. Then we know deep inside that what we have in

front of us is just a free spirit that has chosen to live in a masculine-
or feminine-dominant body. And with that, it will be impossible to
discriminate against the other.

Someone who is 100 percent conscious can't hurt anything or
anyone without first disconnecting themselves from their
consciousness. So, a true healer is connected even though they do
not know everything.

Subject Matter

When we enter this life, we, as spirits, choose a starting point, a
platform from which we can evolve. We choose a body, a family, a
culture, a time in history, and a society from which we can decide to
unfold. Whatever we have chosen to jump into is just a starting
point, not a destination.

Imagine a seed, a piece of wood, or a rock unfolding and
transforming into a flower, a wooden chair, or a statue, respectively.
At its starting point, the subject matter had one expression and
evolved into another.

We have chosen to be a subject matter to unfold our true potential.
Awareness and acceptance of the fact that this is a universal truth
and of the truth in every moment accelerate our unfolding. Suppose
we protest against our origination: the life, the family, and the body
we have given ourselves in this life. In that case, we will call for
lessons to be learned, be wound up in misconceptions, and probably
end up struggling with the circumstances. If we accept the starting
point, the current situation, we liberate ourselves to choose freely in
every moment. Making the best use of the platform we have given

ourselves and how well we manage it will determine our next moment. This moment determines the starting point for the next moment.

This also applies to spirit-full leadership—how we manage our platform and the role we have been given, formally or informally. Leadership, in its basic mechanics, affects how we influence others. If they choose to follow, we are a leader. Leadership, in its mechanics, is not about good or bad. That's a judgment or a preference. In its basics, leadership is solely about whether people follow or not.

The Norwegian author Hans E. Anonsen describes, in my interpretation, leadership as a subject matter evolving into ability in the following way:

"The well-functioning human community is only a potential. The crucial moment in which the team stands or falls is when a leadership role is exercised. It's all about the conscious ability to exercise leadership or the selfish temptation to seek refuge in the power added to the leadership role. Leadership is the ability to inspire and unlock the potential of individuals, teams, and organizations. Whoever wants to make this happen must develop their ability to be a fellow human. What it means to be a fellow is determined solely by how individuals, teams, or organizations can unleash their potential in their presence."

His definition, of course, comes with a preference hidden in the essence of being a fellow being. You could be a dictator and fellow being to your closest friends, unlocking their potential and simultaneously suppressing the public, but that is not what Hans means. He has a preference. I would say that the underlying asset here is a heart-centered, empathic way of being. Humans usually develop this when we accept that we have chosen our own lives and stop being angry, jealous, or trying to dominate others. We start to grow grateful and thankful for living and the opportunity it gives us.

That's why I respect people like John Lennon and Bruce Springsteen. They have done their thing. They have managed their subject matter, unfolded their ability, raised their voice, and expressed their meaning peacefully yet powerfully. They did not try to conquer another country. Quite the opposite, they represented the will of peace and justice and, by that, have conquered the world. They showed their spirit, not being saints but by being transparent with their experiences and flaws. People responded to this and bought their records because they had something to say that appealed to them. Some of their songs will last forever. Just imagine all the people that listen to those words.

Spirit-full leadership can take many forms. It's not about being perfect or a saint. It's about being a fellow human, utilizing the platform we have been given, and choosing to live out a win-win-win way of life. Existence, nature, and the universal truth can guide our navigation if we tune in with them.

The awakened spirit-full leaders' focus is not on protecting their own interests; they just can't. It's impossible because doing so would totally contradict who they are. Instead, they value the common good, the greater good. They dedicate themselves to a mission to benefit not only themselves, their own company, or their country but everyone. They do not see the earth or people as an asset they can exploit for their benefit; they understand it's a temporary loan. They are not hostile or overprotective. They are not naïve to the circumstances; they understand that not everyone has their knowledge or consciousness and that they, in every situation, must be the bigger man who unites and brings harmony. Their focus is to do good!

"Spirit-full leadership is not about imposing one's beliefs on others. It is about creating a space for people to explore their full potential."

~ Unknown

Breaking Out of the
Ordinary World

C onsider the central character in the Hero's Journey narrative framework. He or she is part of what is known as the ordinary world. Luke Skywalker on the planet Tatooine, Dorothy with her family in Kansas, Frodo with the other hobbits in the Shire, and a million other characters from films, books, and comics are examples of characters leaving their ordinary world behind and transforming themselves.

The regular world is a familiar location for the hero. They are unsatisfied, but they are secure. Then there's a call to adventure, when a situation forces them to leave their cushy lives and embark on a journey to become the hero they were born to be.

Embracing the possibilities for becoming a spirited leader involves deeply acknowledging one's inherent talents, consciously utilizing available resources, and strategically leveraging valuable connections. As a spirit-full leader, recognizing these elements forms the foundation of an authentic and impactful leadership style. Acknowledging your talents signifies an awareness of your unique strengths and capabilities, empowering you to lead authentically and purposefully.

Cultivating relationships within your professional and personal spheres provides a support system that can be instrumental in overcoming obstacles and seizing opportunities. A spirit-full leader understands that collaboration and mutual support are valuable assets and essential components in fostering a positive and thriving leadership environment. Thus, being summoned to partake in the adventure is not merely an invitation but a recognition of your potential to embody the principles of spirit-full leadership, combining talent, resources, and connections to lead with purpose and impact.

We could be tempted to cling to the idea that leadership is defined by rank and order. However, your position or title alone does not make you a true leader. Consider how many CEOs worldwide wield enormous influence yet have only a minor impact on their staff. How many bosses aren't even respected by their subordinates? Even the most intelligent and imaginative people often struggle to find their voice. Spirit-full leadership is a skill of influence, something you can use to affect the thoughts, feelings, emotions, and actions of others. A position does not define it, nor is it characterized by academic prowess or natural talent.

Spirit-full leadership is something you embody and develop over time. Many believe it is an innate ability, yet anyone can become a spirit-full leader in anything they choose to master. You could be your company's boss, class teacher, or household head. You might even choose to take charge of your own life. There are many distinct kinds and styles of spirit-full leadership. True spirit-full leadership begins with the ability to control your disappointment. On any worthwhile project, you will face challenges and, more than likely, you will fail. You can become a spirit-full leader if you discover a way to connect with yourself and others, empowering you and your team to surmount any obstacles. You can only transform the ordinary into the extraordinary when you seek to serve something bigger than yourself. In *Star Wars*, Luke Skywalker learns the skills of a Jedi Knight and then confronts his biggest challenge, which is Darth Vader. The spirit-full leader uses their spiritual practice to strengthen their resolve and values to face their challenging roadblocks. Throughout the series, Luke continues his training. Otherwise, he would lose the basis of who he is as a Jedi. The spirit-full leader will also continue to upskill and do their spiritual practice daily, especially if things become hectic. The practice is the foundation of who they are at their core. It's how they remind themselves that they are spiritual beings with a human experience, not vice versa.

Making Clear Decisions

Leading is an important part of being a leader. Managers must be able to manage people well, just as leaders must be able to lead. However, many people do not. They avoid making team-leading decisions since those have consequences. These are leaders you should avoid. No decisions will be made, so they let the situation decide for them, and they can't be held responsible.

It must be decided whether the team devotes time to project A or B, supports customer C or D, or invests in key opportunities E or F. Because no amount of explanation can usually persuade someone to make the better decision, it is up to a leader to "put his life on the line." Great leaders make bold decisions, announcing their decisions and then convincing their team of their reasoning, vision, and rationale for making them.

We now know that the most crucial leadership attribute for a great leader is the ability to lead and make decisions. The next stage is to figure out how we stack up against that leadership attribute. Three questions will assist you in determining if you are leading or not to enable this assessment.

1. In the last four weeks, have you avoided making a decisive decision? From now on, don't put off making a decision.

2. In the last four weeks, have you made a major decision? Good. Make a few more. One per week is a good goal.

3. Have you made any courageous leadership decisions in the last four weeks? Great, please continue.

We've all watched a post-apocalyptic movie or television show such as *The Walking Dead,* where there are no rules, principles, or absolute logic. This is when true leaders emerge. They are prepared to turn left when others demand going right, to keep traveling to find a safer area for the group to sleep, or to create a nighttime watch pattern despite the group's exhaustion.

Would you be the group's leader because you can make difficult decisions? No? So, do you consider yourself a spirit-full leader?

Seeding Spirit-Full Leadership

In the progression of human life, not many experiences can be as discerning and life-changing as a spiritual awakening. Recognizing and staunchly experiencing our spirituality symbolizes a paradigm shift of the highest order. A spiritual awakening has the prospect of capturing the web of reality as we know it and pulls us into a novel existence of mindful development and vigilant realization. As the language suggests, we wake up from everyday reveries (including daily hallucinations and delusions), from the mundane, ego-based responsiveness to a higher reality of spirit. It resembles rising from a deep slumber, coming to light, and seeing the dream for what it is – an illusion we never understood. Spiritual awakening is us releasing the known patterns and learned behaviors that no longer serve our evolution. It's often a painful time to let go of the old and embrace the unknown with hope and faith.

Spirit-full leadership suggests focusing more on people and less on formal positions of power; more on adaptation, positive change, diversity, relationships, collaboration, and encouragement; and less on orthodoxy and control.

Spirituality in leadership is more focused on advancing people as whole individuals. The type who display kindness and empathy to others are bosses, aides, or clients. Spirituality in leadership does not necessitate leaders to stick to a specific religion or to make an effort to influence, persuade, and convert others to follow a definite religious principle. Although leaders who highlight spirituality may base their leadership style on Christianity or another spiritual custom, they may also have non-traditional religious views or may not be advocates of any specific religion.

In the workplace, the spirit-full leader understands the value of workers finding meaning in their work. Therefore, they show authentic compassion for the whole individual, not just the worker. This type of leader also guides then assists others in finding purpose in their work by responding to essential questions such as:

- Who are we as a team?
- Is our work well-intentioned? What is our higher purpose?
- What are our ideals and moral values?

- What will be our legacy?

Hence, the spirit-full leader will go all-out to make the workplace a just community comprising of individuals with collective morals, ideals, and principles.

Considering that a small quantity of empirical research has been conducted about spirituality in the workplace or spirit-full leadership, we cannot exactly establish the gains or costs. However, sufficient theoretical and experiential study has been undertaken to infer numerous possible improvements in integrating a spiritual dimension into leadership. From the supporters' viewpoint, incorporating spirituality into leadership can create a more compassionate domain that provides a sense of community and collective resolve. From the organization's outlook, integrating spirituality in leadership can result in conviction, collaborative support, trust, and dedication among its members, leading to helpful influences on group performance. Nevertheless, spirit-full leadership must not be viewed as a maneuver to produce encouraging outcomes but must be the authentic moral thrust of the leader.

"The spirit-full leader brings out the best in others and encourages them to live authentically and wholeheartedly."

~ Unknown

Awaking Spirit-Full Leadership in Us

—◇०૮⁄ঌ०◇—

S pirit-full leadership is founded on love and a robust and firm ethical attitude. It discards any model of leadership based on intimidation, force, and terror. It places service before self-interest, profoundly pays attention first by encouraging others, instigates confidence and hope by being reliable, truthful, and responsible, and nurtures others to completeness.

The spirit-full leader is a great communicator who actively listens and advocates exchanging ideas, not arguments. This leader uses narratives and metaphors to impart the message that needs to come across to their people.

The spirit-full leader motivates, inspires zeal and tenacity in pursuing the dream, and persuades others to do the same. No intimidation or bullying for this leader. They are a catalyst of transformation and endeavor followers to become leaders. The spirit-full leader helps shape the community's culture, morals, and ideals and serves as a role model for the group.

There are a few qualities you need to awaken your spirit-full leadership. It is not something that you wake up and walk into, it's an inner connection and congruence with oneself that is cultivated over a lifetime. You have to work for it. The difference makers in this world do not just subconsciously get into the place they currently hold. They worked towards it by honing certain qualities, some of which I will share with you now.

Courage

It takes guts to lead on any scale, level, and by formal authority or informal influence. Courage, like leadership, comes in various ways.

Just ponder on it briefly; it could be the valor to do what is required in difficult situations, or the willingness or audacity to be true to your vision, or the ability to stick to your ethics. Courage can also take the shape of service — being the person who is willing to do what is required, to give of yourself, and to serve and contribute to the well-being of others, even though it is unlikely to be returned.

One thing courage is not, however, is being without fear. In fact, fear is an important ingredient for courage. Courage looks like the boldness of bravery, but it transcends that. In whatever form it exhibits itself, here is the essence of what courage feels like when you are in a leadership position.

- Willpower: Courage is having or summoning the mental fortitude to confront something that would otherwise intimidate, derail, or cause you anguish, distress, anxiety, or discomfort. True leaders must be able to demonstrate real strength.

- Choice: Resistance or inflexibility are the most common manifestations of willpower without action. Courage necessitates a willingness to take action. It's flexible, adaptable, and well-intentioned. "I realized courage was not the lack of fear," stated Mark Twain. Indeed, it's deciding to be bigger than fear and taking action.

- Heart: Courage comes from the Latin word 'cor,' which means 'heart.' Courage is frequently illogical, unreasonable, irrational, uncalculated, and even stupid. This is because it doesn't originate in our heads. Your heart is where you get your courage. Passion, caring, and conviction are the driving forces behind it.

So, whether you're calling your courage or encouraging someone else's (the word encourage means 'to give courage to'), the first leadership trait is about mobilizing the inner strength to act — directed and inspired by the heart. It's a difference-maker's distinctive feature.

Compassion

Compassion and *leadership* are rarely used in the same sentence. Compassion is frequently perceived as a 'soft' or even passive attribute. We equate compassion, which is easily confused with empathy, as a response to others' pain: an ability to sympathize, feel care, and show concern.

Conversely, leadership is frequently associated with strong, even tough, action — and results! Yet, as a leadership quality, compassion has been displayed by numerous greats throughout history and Stefan and I will expand on these leaders later on.

Compassion as a leadership trait harkens to the true sense of the word - an emotion in reaction to another or condition that elicits and inspires constructive, positive action to alleviate or ameliorate the situation.

This is where toughness does, indeed, come into play. Not hard-heartedness, but the kind of tough action needed to actually make a difference, to thrive.

Let's consider this: What would compassionate leadership mean? What would it look like? What would be its effect on performance, productivity, and results?

It would most likely involve a greater focus on people, greater social consciousness, increased corporate citizenship, improved ethics, increased stewardship, and a dedicated focus on the "triple bottom line": people, planet, and profit, or even collaborative solutions.

That is what compassion aspires to awaken in leaders. The ability to relate to others – even, and sometimes especially, those who are unique, maybe even in opposition – and the desire to behave in a way that surpasses differences or issues and promotes meaningful outcomes.

I was trying to contact one of my video editors regarding an urgent matter recently. The period leading into Christmas can become hectic, but I was still somewhat surprised when he hadn't responded to my direct communication for over an hour. Usually, he communicates within five to ten minutes. I instinctively called his cell phone but received no response. Although he works from home, his wife takes care of their four-month-old baby girl during the day.

Turns out that his daughter was crying incessantly with his wife unable to calm their baby. She asked my editor for support. So he spent an hour calming her down until she drifted asleep. Despite the fact that we had a fast-approaching deadline and external pressures, granting my employee grace was the most humane thing to do. When you have a committed team player who's bought into the vision and collectible outcomes, what choice do you have other than empathizing with them?

Compassion is a leadership trait based on a desire to understand, the ability to relate, and the desire, urge, and felt responsibility and commitment to act. It's a mission to thrive, as Maya Angelou put it.

Commitment

Commitment is a pivotal trait for a spirit-filled leader to embrace and embody in their leadership journey. It extends beyond promises, commitments, or guarantees; it entails a profound dedication to hear, genuinely listen, and deeply comprehend people actively. A spirit-full leader's commitment transcends the superficial, aiming to cultivate a leadership style grounded in a comprehensive and integrated perspective, with the overarching goal of achieving outcomes that surpass the interests of any single party.

This level of commitment requires a genuine readiness to confront challenges head-on. It involves a deliberate intention and unwavering devotion to acknowledge and truly understand many often conflicting ideas. A spirit-full leader committed to this process recognizes the importance of embracing diverse perspectives, viewing them not as obstacles but as opportunities for growth and collaboration. By committing to this approach, leaders foster an environment where collaboration and understanding are valued, contributing to a more inclusive and effective leadership style that resonates with the team's spirit.

Connection

Given humanity's nature, living in a society free of tension, anxiety, and insecurity—with true communication lines between team members kept open—may be a pipe dream that will never be achieved. Isn't it past time for us to start putting this call into action?

Leadership encourages us to continue working to build relationships that allow for open communication channels among people.

It begins with you and me—how well we connect and communicate with one another. It's all about reintroducing human relations into our conversational effectiveness—the ability to "relate" rather than transact with others. This is the responsibility of the leader.

Conditioning

Conditioning comes in three forms when it comes to the qualities that will help you awaken and grow your inner leader:

Outer-Conditioning: What happens to us (or has happened to us) shapes our learned response. It's easy to succumb to external circumstances, especially when unpleasant or we don't control them.

This can lead to "learned helplessness," a victim mentality that can overpower and suffocate the inner leader's ability (or hope) to make a difference.

As a result, it is incumbent upon us to carefully analyze our external environments—and to pick what we allow in and the story we make about it in our own minds with present, attention, and purposeful thought.

Simply put, we must use emotional intelligence to maintain social awareness that will allow us to continue to lead.

Other conditioning is what we encounter in our interactions with others and which informs our judgments, opinions, connections, and interpersonal effectiveness.

It's a form of conditioning in which we believe we know the other person after a while. Or we believe we understand what people like them do, say, think, or reason.

At that point, we become blind to their contribution, our connection to them, and perhaps even a barrier to it.

Awakening the leader within us requires remaining open and responsive to others, knowledgeable but not prejudiced or conditioned by our previous experiences. This enables us to continue to see, hear, and feel people for who they are, while also energizing their potential.

Inner conditioning is something we choose, produce, and nurture from within ourselves to form new habits, learn, grow, and develop.

This final training requires us to know the 80-20 rule.

We recognize that our outer and other conditioning is likely pulling, influencing, and magnetizing a good 80 percent or more of our time and attention.

Real results, on the other hand, come from devoting 20% (or less) of our time to inner reflection, learning, and growth, according to the leader within. We frequently discover that spending 20% of our time on the inner produces 80+ % of our results, both with respect to outer people and situations—never the other way around.

This implies that we must devote time to self-awareness, management, regeneration, rest, reading, caring for our health and well-being, learning, and leadership development.

Leaders must practice "Sharpening the saw," as Stephen R. Covey describes in his book *The 7 Habits of Highly Effective People.* "It means protecting and strengthening the greatest thing you have— YOU," he explains.

Conditioning, especially regarding leadership, is similar to becoming an athlete. It's about taking your leadership role, responsibility, privilege, and gift seriously and optimizing yourself to give your best to people in your life and the world. It's the mentality of an Olympian when it comes to your spirit-full leader.

Embodying All of Who You Are

To be seen as a true leader you need to find your authentic voice, dare to face your fears, and show your vulnerability. Let me pose a question to you... Who is truly in charge of you? We are not talking about your boss, not your coach, not your mentor, not your partner, and certainly not anybody else. But on the inside, from within, who guides you?

Of course, the answer is you. Whether you've chosen to embrace self-leadership completely or you've opted to remain in a passive role, allowing everything around you to direct your path, you are the one who makes the final decisions in your life.

Your inner leader is a tremendous force, and connecting with it allows you to generate joy, meaning, and success in many areas of your life, including leadership. The best leaders—those who bring forth the best in others and achieve big-picture success—recognize that strong leadership begins within. They understand that the first stage is to find personal peace and clarity to meet everyone else as their ideal selves.

So, how can you cultivate inner leadership? How can you engage the part of you that intuitively understands what's best for you? It begins within, as with most transitions.

Leaders with well-developed inner leaders nearly always respond effectively—not with fixes, but in a manner that opens the doors to new possibilities, puts people at ease and motivates growth. Either they've put in the effort to embrace their inner leader completely, or they're lucky enough to have never lost touch in the first place. As a result, they can respond to practically any circumstance calmly and clearly.

Everything you do affects others around you. You are not in charge of how they show up or react, but you are in charge of how you show up and react. That is the magnitude of your influence. You are making a conscious decision in your influence when you turn up from your highest self.

You are significantly less aware of your impact on others and yourself when you lead from your lower self—that is when you are detached from your inner self. This causes resentment and judgment, both of others and yourself.

The inner leader is the side of you that trusts in and is committed to living out your values and purpose. They want you to succeed and will hold you in their arms with unconditional acceptance and love while guiding you with insight, empathy, fortitude, vision, and confidence. These traits are inherent in you; nonetheless, it is up to you to bring them to the fore. Allowing your higher self to guide the way is a conscious choice.

As leaders, we must be mindful of our words and frequently become entangled in office politics. However, regardless of your company's present culture, there is always room for truth, and your inner leader can help.

It's not easy to speak your mind in a professional context, but it's well worth it. It helps you become a stronger, more approachable leader who can hold a safe space for others while empowering them to speak their truth. The trick is to connect with your inner leader before engaging in any conversation in which you must speak your truth, especially if you believe it will be difficult.

A recent encounter with a persistent client was a valuable lesson when developing my inner leader. The constant barrage of WhatsApp messages from the client disrupted the delicate balance of my workflow. Despite my attempts to provide information through email, the client insisted on using WhatsApp, creating a pattern that impeded productivity and led to disorganization as redundant requests poured in.

Navigating this situation, I recognized the importance of asserting healthy boundaries to protect my own well-being while maintaining a positive client relationship. It became crucial to communicate effectively, balancing assertiveness with empathy. I addressed the issue as diplomatically as possible, explaining the advantages of email and suggesting delegating specific tasks to the client's virtual assistant. Though initially offended, the client eventually embraced a compromise, finding a middle ground that incorporated email and WhatsApp.

This experience highlighted the significance of developing one's inner leader, highlighting the ability to voice needs, set boundaries, and foster effective communication. The client relationship endured and strengthened by navigating this challenge with grace and assertiveness. This episode underscored that developing your inner leader involves managing external relationships and prioritizing self-respect and well-being in pursuing professional success.

When you try to tell your truth, you hand over control to your best, most empowering self, and you gain trust in your inner leader. The connection to your inner leader strengthens as greater truths come to light.

"A true spirit-full leader listens deeply asks meaningful questions, and helps others connect with their inner wisdom."

~ Unknown

Clarity Is Empowerment

I feel that now, more than ever, people crave inner peace—not just the possibility of inner peace. Today, people desire a life bursting with love and overflowing with companionship. We now abhor lives jam-packed with anxiety and desolation. Instead, we want communities that genuinely have our back, not those that allow the mighty to prey on us.

Admittedly, these are interesting, albeit dangerous, times, but we are in a fascinating and thought-provoking era. Unfortunately, we also live in a culture of self-preoccupation, selfies, and egotistical social media posts.

Most people lack self-awareness due to the busyness of everyday life. Michael Beckwith, the founder of Agape International Spiritual Center and one of the stars of *The Secret*, believes that many people suffer from intention deficit disorder in today's world.

Reality-wise, many grew up in an atmosphere where thinking or engaging in conversations about ourselves was censured or disliked. In those times, reflecting on our inner selves was considered self-absorption.

But I sincerely think that the spiritual life requires us to do that. The type of self-reflection people hastily condemn as self-absorption is the kind that can lead us to eye-opening self-awareness.

We must examine our actions, habits, decisions, and plans to see what is and is not leading us to our goals and full potential. Then, with mindful reflection, we can expose our need for rest, engage ourselves more in our communities, or toss away a practice that no longer serves us.

"Self-examination is the process of accountability to your soul. It is far better to 'become' your truth than to speak it. Self-examination is the practice of becoming your truth."
~ *Caroline Myss*

Self-awareness is the path to seeing the needs of our fellow men. How can we carry out the work of caring for others if we don't understand ourselves and our gifts and needs? The cliché advice about putting on our own oxygen mask before helping others is necessary. But then again, to engage and accomplish this reflective task, we need to be modest and overcome our propensity for self-absorption.

Self-absorption is always directed and focused on ourselves. On the other hand, self-awareness is for the service of others. The lifeblood of inner spiritual maturity is to help us better serve and share love with others.

Spirituality entails a sense of connection outside ourselves. It comprises our ideals, the gist of our lives, and what drives us. Our spiritual well-being is what stirs us, makes us bounce from fear to courage, and causes us to become the best versions of ourselves. Our spirit is where our profound values and character are positioned. It's that part of us that senses, constructs value judgments, and contemplates and deliberates our connection to other people, our ethical standards, and the world. Hence, spirituality is viewed in terms of a search. It is a continuing expedition to seek answers and see things in novel and diverse ways. It also means discovering and establishing our purpose in life and staying aligned with it.

> *"We spend so much time asking God to cure*
> *us of our hardships.*
> *But we never stop to consider that our*
> *hardships are curing us."*
> ~ *Yasmin Mogahed*

In spirit-full leadership, the common misconception that talents and abilities are innate becomes a transformative opportunity for growth. Contrary to the belief that we are born with fixed qualities, spirit-full leaders recognize the dynamic nature of creativity and individual talents. Much like the muscles in the body requiring exercise for optimal function, each individual's latent skills and abilities need to be consciously practiced and nurtured to reach their full potential. In the spirit-full leadership paradigm, it is understood that the development and enhancement of creativity and talents are not predetermined but can be awakened through intentional and mindful cultivation.

Just as one dedicates time to physical exercise through activities like jogging or hitting the gym to sculpt their body, a spirit-full leader believes it is equally imperative to awaken dormant skills and abilities. The process involves a deliberate and continuous effort to practice and refine these latent qualities. In the spirit-full leadership ethos, the belief persists that creativity, much like a muscle, can be honed through consistent and purposeful engagement. This perspective challenges the notion of fixed abilities, fostering an environment where leaders actively seek to awaken and amplify the latent potential within themselves and their teams, contributing to a culture of continuous improvement and innovation.

- While self-actualization cannot be accomplished overnight, it can be achieved. These strategies may help:

Attain a sense of direction and achieve a purposeful life

We're in trouble when life appears like a long, drawn-out marathon without any finish line. But if we work hard to tune in to the voice of our soul and strive to be focused on our desires, we have bigger chances of leading a life of contentment, self-actualization, and happiness.

Without the disruptions and commotions of daily life, we can become entrenched in the knowledge that we have control and are so powerful that we can achieve any dream within our spirit. With this knowledge, we can hone whatever sleeping talent or ability is buried deep in us.

- By silencing our thoughts and acclimatizing ourselves to our souls, we can master our capacity to manifest anything. When we have discovered the easiest way to find tranquility, the invitation is there to open fully to our true nature, even when life gets muddled and messy. When we have silenced ourselves, lucidity comes naturally and inevitably. Thus, being alert and observant of what rises to the front of our minds as the clatter and disorder diminish is essential.

Make way for our innermost passions

By stepping away, we can easily tap into our innermost potential and desires. Without being whisked into the endless whirl of pushing toward perfection, we become cognizant of our choices every second of the day and how those options mold our persona. This is the way of the spirit-full leader in the 21st century.

- Nature provides us with a chance to acclimate to the wisdom of our bodies, so we'll know immediately if a choice we've made has supported our true selves or not. We will discover the best and most efficient way to open ourselves up to the richness of the cosmos. I invite you to get intentional about the reality you really desire to create for yourself. Think from a paradigm of limitless potential and trust yourself to tap into unlimited possibilities. Allow yourself to go within for the answers you seek.

Release restrictive views

- In an age where limitations and judgments are prevalent, destructive and off-putting opinions can unsettle our capacity to become who we are fully. Stepping away from these judgments and confusion games, we are confronted with only ourselves and the vastness inside us. We reveal our intrinsic capabilities and talents that could unwrap our greatest gifts by liberating ourselves from these restrictive views. Similarly, we need to learn to relinquish the habit of condemning and judging ourselves and others by altering harmful thoughts towards ourselves and abandoning critical views of other people.

Toss away hoarded anxieties

While fear and stress are potent tools in certain instances, they should not be mainstays in our lives. Instead of amassing them inside us, they're best tossed away because they can hamper our ability to appreciate life and can surely inflict mayhem on our physical and mental conditions.

- A few ways to prevent the buildup of fear and stress are to escape into nature, live for the present, and let go of spiritual lumps such as fretfulness, hopelessness, disquiet, and resistance to change, all of which can lead to tension and devastating pressure in our everyday existence. The invitation is there to liberate ourselves from the prison of our previous conditioning and march out from the roles or narratives that no longer serve us. Finally, we need to master practices that can enable us to embrace uncertainties and change, as these are fruitful grounds for creativity and self-determination.

Develop reflective and introspective practices

As mentioned, embracing meditative and introspective practices becomes integral to establishing a robust foundation for spiritual life. These deliberate and mindful exercises serve as transformative tools, allowing spirit-full leaders to cultivate and nurture a method that fosters a profound connection with their authentic selves, even amidst life's chaos and disruptions. The essence of these practices lies in mastering the intentional discernment of life-centered, present-moment mindfulness.

For spirit-full leaders, the ability to navigate complexities and challenges, whether perceived or real, is profoundly enhanced through intentional discernment. By anchoring themselves in the present moment, these leaders develop a heightened awareness that dismantles complications and stumbling blocks, creating a space for clarity and purpose. The focus shifts towards a collective commitment to doing good, extending beyond individual aspirations to encompass the well-being of all humanity.

As spirit-full leaders align their purposes with a broader perspective, they realize that dreams and aspirations are not solitary endeavors but interconnected threads weaving into the fabric of a collective vision. The power of intentional discernment, coupled with meditative practices, accelerates the manifestation of these dreams. In the spirit-full leadership narrative, the fusion of mindfulness, introspection, and a commitment to collective good catalyzes a rapid materialization of visions and aspirations, contributing to a world where positive change becomes both a possibility and a tangible reality.

> *"Learning emerges from discovery, not directives;*
> *reflection, not rules; possibilities, not prescriptions;*
> *diversity, not dogma; creativity and curiosity,*
> *not conformity and certainty;*
> *and meaning, not mandates."*
> *~ Stephanie Marshall*

"Spirit-full leadership is about cultivating a sense of unity, connection and harmony among all beings."

~ Unknown

Breaking Out

A re you one of those people who gets up at the same time every morning, shuttles back and forth using the same method of transportation, and goes to the same environment to spend eight to nine hours each day doing the same type of work? Getting fed up and unsatisfied with that kind of existence isn't difficult. The feeling then is that of being stuck, often to a point of no return.

It doesn't have to be this way.

I believe that every day lent to us is a renewed opportunity to change our lives. Growing up, I was taught not to give up on things worth fighting or living for. This is easy to believe but not easy to do. If we wish to become part of a better world, we need to start by going beyond our expectations.

We need to be willing to look into our innermost selves every day and push past our limitations. Many times, we'll find that in doing this, we are required to step out of our comfort zones. While this activity demands us to push through our limits and confront our doubts and worries, what exists on the other side of that voyage is truly incredible: a life beyond what we ever imagined.

American writer and historian James Truslow Adams once said, "There are obviously two educations. One should teach us how to make a living and the other how to live."

I remember a time in my life when I wasn't sure what I wanted to do anymore. I had my second landscape gardening business for almost five years and the business was doing quite well. The problem was that my passion for the work had waned after sixteen years in the industry. I felt a calling to pursue a greater purpose in life, but I didn't know what that could be.

I had already begun a spiritual practice, and I had done a number of personal development programs, including working with a couple of counselors to process certain traumatic experiences in my life.

When we live life on autopilot, three things can happen; we wander and bum around without a vibrant, interesting, and optimistic reaction to stimulate us, we get trapped in a pothole of outdated, unproductive ways of looking at and doing things, or, we are snared in a surge of urgent matters we call being busy, matters that are usually temporary and fixated on countering, instead of proactively building, the future.

These can lead us towards life living us rather than us living life. It's a straightforward place to escape from but so challenging.

Come to think of it, we can choose how we look at life's responsibilities, chances, challenges, trials, and misfortunes. How we get into something substantially influences how it goes and where it ends up. We can fight, resist, and make excuses, or drag ourselves from task to task, spiritless and putting out a lackluster performance. We can also go through the motions and pretend we're doing something and liking it. We can smile (or smirk) and put up with it to get it over and done with. Or, we can engage positively. We can embrace whatever we need to accept with openness, infusing energy, concentration, dedication, and, if possible, a sense of excitement and pleasure. With this disposition, we can bring the extraordinary into something very ordinary. This is spirit-full leadership at its core.

The Power of Choice

Life is full of situations that push us to make choices, weigh our options, and choose the lesser evil. Some choices can be very simple, such as what color of dress to wear or what to have for dinner. Others can be slightly more complicated, like choosing between becoming a carnivore or a vegetarian. And some choices need a lot of serious thought, like what career to choose or whether to get married. Good decision-making skills are an invaluable asset in life, no matter how big the decision.

At times, we arrive at logical decisions. However, sometimes, we make decisions based on emotions or the absence of verifiable facts, leading to fewer choices and vague decisions.

As humans, though, we all want to make the finest decisions in life—whether they are as mundane as deciding whether to date someone, doggedly aim for the manager's seat, or finish that DIY project that commenced several weeks ago.

How do we allow our innermost cognizance or spirit to guide us when making decisions? Can we avoid letting our ego interfere when we make our choices? And how important is it to know if we have been guided by our innermost cognizance or if it's the negative ego working and ruling over our minds?

Jona Genova, founder and CEO of Samadhi for Peace and Reiki Collective, said, "Living in truth and integrity will always lead to spirit-based decisions." Further, she said that "Ego decisions will leave us empty because they rely upon outer affirmation. Spiritual decisions rest on something deeper, truer."

Thus, when we find ourselves at many of life's intersections and are firmly in doubt about which way to go, the insights below can help allow our inner selves to guide us toward our most authentic path.

Spirit Vs. Ego

Let's learn how the spirit and ego differ in how each makes us feel. The ego is like our internal nitpicker, our faultfinder who wants to confine us in a distress-based reality. The ego is opposed to embarrassment or humiliation and expressly detests being wrong. The ego stops us from moving away from obsolete ways, destructive habits, damaging patterns, and comfortable practices that keep us dormant, idle, playing safe, and looking at ourselves as not enough.

This ego is that little voice inside our heads asking us, *Who are we anyway?* It leads us to think of all the nastiest situations before we make a decision. This naturally leads us to falter and have misgivings about our instincts and intrinsic capabilities. While the ego may keep us safe, it keeps us from doing bigger things, acting out our aspirations, and discovering a more expansive way of living. The ego is condemnatory, controlling, cynical, and reproachful.

On the other hand, the inner spirit is more open and richer, bursting with love and overflowing with possibilities. Our spirit is designed to continuously direct us to the decision that mirrors the highest good for ourselves and others. It aids us in learning through compassion and growth. When we're strongly linked to our spirit and inner selves, we can reconcile with the love and internal guidance within us all.

"The spirit-full leader understands that true power lies in surrendering to the divine and trusting in the universe's wisdom."

~ Unknown

Tapping Into Our Spirit

————————⟡————————

H ow can we tap into our spirit? How do we listen to it? How can we determine that it isn't our ego talking?

"I find that there is a nervousness when the ego is talking... Spirit feels unshakable, certain, light," says Lisa Genova in her book *Still Alice*. Genova is an American neuroscientist and author best known for her novels that explore neurological disorders and their impact on individuals and their families. In *Still Alice* she tells the story of a Harvard professor who is diagnosed with early-onset Alzheimer's disease. The quote reflects the character's introspective thoughts on the contrast between the nervousness associated with the ego and the spirit's unshakable, certain, and light nature.

Practical scenarios allow us to tap into our inner spirit and make decisions aligned with our authentic selves. Consider deciding whether to take a job that entails relocating across the country. The ego may interject with concerns about leaving established friendships and a reliable income source, questioning the worthiness of the new job. However, in this scenario, a spirit-full leader would first turn inward and inquire whether the job aligns with their dream career. The spirit asks, "Does the prospect of working in a new environment feel thrilling?" It introduces a sense of positivity, fervor, and optimism about the future.

Reflecting the spirit in our lives necessitates introspection and a series of crucial inquiries. Are we connected daily or creating opportunities to connect with our inner spirit? Do we balance work and play or succumb to work pressures until burnout? Have we immersed ourselves in the rejuvenating embrace of nature, deliberately steering away from distractions? Most importantly, are we actively cultivating the ability to love ourselves and others unconditionally?

Consistently maintaining this level of awareness enables spirit-full leaders to make decisions effortlessly grounded in their authentic selves. Such decisions ensure that they are transparent and beneficial, not just to the individual making them but also to the broader spectrum of humanity. In the context of spirit-full leadership, staying connected with one's spirit becomes a guiding principle, ensuring that decisions are aligned with personal aspirations and contribute positively to the collective well-being.

In spirit-full leadership, the imperative is to let our core values steer our decisions, becoming the guiding force that shapes our choices. This approach does not negate the importance of other facets in the decision-making process; it underscores the need to integrate our fundamental principles into the entire framework seamlessly.

When a spirit-full leader faces a business issue, the inquiry transcends the traditional "Will this make money?" to a more profound "Is this aligned with our values?" The subsequent consideration of financial viability is still relevant, but the priority is to align with core principles. If the answer is negative, the spirit-full leader must seek an alternative, grounding decisions in a harmonious coexistence with values. The underlying logic is to live and work congruently with these values, fostering a life one can be proud of rather than a life marked by regret.

In the framework of spirit-full leadership, pausing to reflect on our values becomes paramount. Without this introspective breather, decisions are more likely to be driven solely by the immediate information. Such an approach, devoid of the guiding light of values, becomes a certain recipe for remorse in the future.

Spirit-full leaders recognize the necessity of this contemplative pause, ensuring that every decision reflects their core principles. By infusing the decision-making process with the essence of their values, spirit-full leaders pave the way for a purposeful and meaningful journey, both in their personal lives and within the realms of leadership.

Our Best Selves

The scenarios of job interviews and dates serve as poignant reminders of the conscious effort to project qualities like self-assurance, diligence, and professionalism. Individuals entering job interviews strategically showcase problem-solving skills and interpersonal abilities, aiming to align their actions with societal expectations of success. Similarly, in the context of a date, people endeavor to conceal nervousness and project an image of composure, emphasizing qualities such as gentleness and humor.

However, the essence of spirit-full leadership encourages a deeper reflection: why limit the exhibition of our best selves to specific occasions? What if we committed to being our authentic and best selves every day instead of selectively showcasing our qualities?

In pursuing spirit-full leadership, the emphasis shifts from occasional demonstrations of excellence to a daily commitment to personal growth and authenticity. By aligning actions with values and virtues consistently, we elevate ourselves and contribute positively to the world around us. The spirit-full leader recognizes that greatness is not a sporadic achievement but a result of continuous efforts to be the best version of oneself, fostering a culture of authenticity, growth, and positive impact. Therefore, if we live each day ready to demonstrate the qualities below, we'll surely be on our way to greatness.

Broadmindedness

Admittedly, we're innately judgmental every once in a while. To avoid being ensnared in this frame of mind and instead open up to people, we need to get to know them and understand why they do what they do. We should never disregard that other people come from diverse backgrounds and have different value systems. They may look very different from us, but that does not mean they do not merit the respect or compassion that everybody else gets. We can make it a rule of thumb to open our minds to modern concepts, fresh ideas, and new people. The spirit-full leader of today has a global perspective from life experiences, reading, travel, hobbies, and a general passion for living in wonder.

Empathy

It's all too easy to become entangled in the intricacies of our lives and challenges. However, a crucial aspect of cultivating a spirit-full approach is constantly reminding ourselves of the vast world beyond our personal sphere—a world where countless people, whom we may never encounter, grapple with forms of suffering that remain alien to our experiences. In the midst of concern about weight gain, job loss, or the emotional upheaval of a divorce, a spirit-full leader pauses to reflect on their fortunes and the hardships others endure globally.

This introspection becomes a catalyst for transformative action. A spirit-full leader understands that true greatness lies in transcending self-centered concerns and embracing compassion for the broader human experience. Instead of wallowing in personal challenges, the leader focuses on contributing meaningfully to others' lives.

Fundamentally, spirit-full leadership encourages a paradigm shift from self-absorption to a genuine concern for the well-being of others. By adopting this empathetic stance, leaders acknowledge the shared humanity that connects us and actively contribute to improving the global community. The spirit-full leader embodies the belief that, in fostering compassion and selflessness, one not only enriches the lives of others but also experiences a profound sense of fulfillment and purpose.

Kindness

Kindness is a powerful and transformative force, with a simple smile as its direct and far-reaching manifestation. The spirit-full leader understands the profound impact of a genuine smile extended to the newspaper delivery person, the neighborhood ice cream vendor, or the neighbor heading to work.

It's a recognition that kindness can be woven into the fabric of daily interactions—complimenting friends, reaching out to parents, and wishing people well. The spirit-full leader acknowledges that beneath the surface, everyone may be navigating challenges and that sometimes, all it takes is a smile, attention, and a contagious positive outlook to make a difference.

Kindness, in the context of spirit-full leadership, transcends grand gestures and extravagant charity contributions. It encompasses the simple yet profound acts of holding the door for someone, assisting an older woman with her groceries, or offering a homeless person the benefit of the doubt and a couple of dollars. These actions are tangible manifestations of kindness, illustrating that generosity can be expressed in actions and thoughts. The spirit-full leader envisions a world where small acts of kindness, multiplied across seven billion people, have the potential to significantly improve our collective existence.

Love as an Action

Love is necessary, whether it's in the office or at home. When you spend significant time with people, you are bound to form a connection. Conversely, a person who resists this kind of sentiment may be perceived as unapproachable.

Love alone may not be enough as an action, but it does shift the balance over time. Results may take longer, but the spiritual bond it creates with the followers will improve team efficiency and increase trust.

> *"I believe that unarmed truth and unconditional love will have the final word in reality. This is why right, temporarily defeated, is stronger than evil triumphant."*
> *~ Martin Luther King Jr.*

Once love is embraced, it needs to be made actionable. Love can be a tool to drive towards a common goal. The first step is to have high expectations; you feel love for your team, and as a result, you will expect them to make substantial achievements. A spirit-full leader shows love by expecting followers to strive for perfection.

This does not necessarily mean you will need to be easy on your team and the tasks at hand. Of course, everyone will need to work efficiently. But by trusting your team's capabilities, you show your love and confidence that they can do a great job.

Connection is also vital for your team. Especially among millennials, there is an intense desire to feel part of a team. They want to know that they matter—that you care for them.

Encouragement is also an act of love. Spirit-full leaders are positioned at the front, looking at the things ahead of them—so their job is to inspire their subordinates to follow where they lead. Encouragement is not done simply by pointing out individual shortcomings. While this may work temporarily, it won't work forever. Instead, the focus should be on what the team can achieve together. This will reduce frustration and allow for an even deeper connection.

For love to be a value, it must be a genuine action, not a tactic. For instance, at the end of a project, a caring leader will ask the other team members if they need any support and will take a real interest in them, even asking about an individual's personal life.

Keep in Mind

Meeting ourselves wherever we are. If we feel sluggish, lackluster, dazed, distracted, and nervous, we should immediately accept that this is where we are now. Then, consider asking ourselves what would help us take one step in a more logical or peaceful direction.

Ultimately, acknowledging our emotions and being aware does not necessarily signify being happy. Feeling negative emotions, such as loneliness or terror, is not a crime. We need to recognize that a vigorous emotional life is full and round and that all feelings, whether positive or negative, are all parts of the whole that is ourselves.

The biggest question that needs to be asked is this: *What would it be like to incorporate and venerate all the parts of our human nature, live perceptively in this corporeal reality, and be mindful that we are a non-material spirit entity?*

"Leadership is the catalytic gift that energizes, directs, and empowers all the other gifts."

~ Bill Hybels

A Call for Love

―――――∽∘↶↷∘↶∘―――――

A book is most often a result of the era in which it was created. Writing a book about leadership in our time without mentioning the current world's evolution would be like walking blindfolded. Even though spirit-full leadership is timeless, leadership is always about the present. Leadership is an effect of a person acting in the present. Therefore, this chapter reflects on the spirit-full leader's way of taking on a situation to understand what the situation wants to tell us. It's about zooming out and using the broader perspective's mindset that people like Socrates, Lao Tze, and Marcus Aurelius have practiced and taught us about since ancient times.

Whether we like to see it or not, the world's current evolution is manufactured, as most situations are, and have always been, even though we might want to blame some outer circumstance for reality. We humans have caused it ourselves; we can also change it. For example, the last years have had the global pandemic with lockdowns, the war in Syria, the war in Ukraine, the economic situation, the climate change, and the world crisis; these are all man-made. Nature has had little to do with it; it only reacts and responds to our actions. The problem is caused by human consciousness, activities, and decisions or lack of decisions, which is not the first time. History, in many ways, keeps repeating itself.

We should know that COVID-19 is just a virus; it does not want anything from us and doesn't want to hurt or make us sick. It's not an enemy we can defeat; it's just a virus. The virus does not spread itself; it's humans that spread the virus. But, unfortunately, just like how we spread wars, climate effects, and economic disasters, or when we spread wealth, health, and innovation in this giant creation of life, we live and act out of fear rather than compassion.

The current circumstances challenge humanity to broaden our conscious understanding of our interactions, relationships with each other and nature, and how we shape our lives and the world around us.

It's a call to open up, not shut down. Closing borders, shutting schools, and mandating remote work may be pragmatic necessities, and I trust the government's judgment in these matters. However, as humans often do, we seek an external enemy to rally against. We unite in a collective effort to prevail against this chosen adversary. Our reactions tend to mimic one another. The real call is to open our hearts, to remain heart-connected, and to think with our hearts rather than our minds. This is an approach we can adopt (and many have) even when physically distant or confined to our homes.

We should remember that without a victim, the aggressor will soon be without opponents. Remember Astrid Lindgren's words earlier in the book. The Zen master does not attack; he waits and listens to the situation. Acting to change the direction of the energy. That's how a Spirit-full leader works. They do not close borders and try to make benefits only for their own country or people who comply with their rules. They know that cooperation is the best way to overcome any situation. Some would argue that this is naïve, more complex than that, and, yes, it is more complicated, but in reality, and truth, it is straightforward. Lay down the arrogance and fear and act upon a clearer view of things. Change happens at the moment when human minds turn around the key and work inside in a new way.

The situation shows us our co-dependence on each other and that we should take co-dependent responsibility for our direction instead of only watching our interests. It shows us that humans are co-dependent on each other and co-creating on all levels. It is one of the highest and finest levels of a mutual relationship, where parts are co-dependent of each other in a mutual understanding and sharing.

Before we close borders, lock down societies, and create significant crises, one could have hoped that the world leaders should have sat down together and tried to understand the situation. Maybe they did, I don't know, but it does not seem like they did. It looks like we acted as copycats; if we did not conform to the same actions as the others, we could look bad in the media and, God forbid, perhaps not be elected in the next election. The question is whether we want to solve this situation together or if we want to protect our interests.

One can think of who will take responsibility for the situation. Will China do that? What about the war in Syria or Ukraine? Will Russia and Syria take responsibility and pay for the consequences of keeping the war going, refugees dying in the Mediterranean trying to escape, refugee camps, broken families, etc., and the war in Ukraine? Will Russia take responsibility and pay for all the damage that it does to the world? Will the USA take responsibility for their actions, or will Brazil take responsibility for the decomposition of the rainforest, and what effects will that have on climate change?

Will we, as a global community, take responsibility for climate change? Are those in charge of all the misery taking responsibility, and is anyone confronting those responsible? Many at the political level seem to play a role in a political-religious game, saying that we must negotiate. Negotiate about what? As previously mentioned, Mother Earth does not negotiate.

All the corporate leaders in the world make money from others' misery or the newly coined term: "greedflation." Nowadays, prices are raised just because it is possible, not because it is necessary. Possibly because we do not make a bottom line that is as big as expected. This is not spirit-full leadership.

However, the situation also shows that many have heeded the call, showcasing human interaction at its best. For instance, consider all the volunteers who worked in medical care during the pandemic and innovations for cleaning the ocean of plastic.

The world is simultaneously taking quantum leaps in the utilization of technology, and politics has shown that under crisis circumstances, they can make decisions and take actions that they, under normal circumstances, would debate for years without taking any steps.

So, why must it become a crisis to increase our consciousness?

Understanding Responsibility

To understand this, we need to understand responsibility.

All leadership comes with a responsibility given by existence, a universal responsibility very natural, not to perform but to be. Anybody who exercises a role as a leader, and that is every person who walks this Earth, either in a formal position or an informal role, is appointed this responsibility. Everyone is, at some point, a leader, and the illusion of the leader being a shepherd for a flock of sheep who needs direction is outdated. We are all leaders, at least for our lives, and responsible for our being and actions.

The responsibility is to put ourselves to service for existence, the universe, and ourselves. As a tiny species, we believe we are more critical to Earth than we are. Our life is not even a blink of an eye compared to Earth's or the universe's history.

What about if the gifts, the talents you've got, were a loan? Something you got and which meaning is that we should put ourselves into service. We have been given a gift, life, as a loan, and existence is waiting for us to make good use of it. This applies to all resources you have, all relations, money, and assets, and it's just a loan.

That's why leadership is about humbleness, serving, and listening, not dictating, competing, directing, or supervising.

There are some magic questions; the primary one is to listen to the situation and ask.

What does the situation want to tell us? What does it want us to be? What does it want us to do?

When I asked that question about the current world situation, I got the response that the problem is a call for love and bold decisions. Think with your heart, not your mind.

The boldest decision is not to do actions outside ourselves, like restricting physical human interaction or sacking people; our gross margins are not in line with what the owners demand, and that's a reactive action due to the circumstances. No, the boldest and most courageous move is to take a long, good look in the mirror, take a big breath, and turn inside to see which part of ourselves we allow to control our actions and start to be aware of that part. Is it fear, greed, envy, survival, or compassion, peace, joy, and love that we let control our actions? This goes for everyone, whether we act as president or anything else. First of all, we are humans on this green planet.

It's time to make a bold decision, a long look in the mirror to see our actions and what they lead to. Every time is an excellent time to learn about ourselves, expand our consciousness, take new measures, and create the future that we want, not repeating structures and patterns that are useless to us.

The situation calls for heart-centered, spirit-full leadership; it calls for love.

The Power of the Heart

The power of the heart is central to the human constitution and is tremendous, where the greatest potential lies for us to connect to and unfold.

Spirit-full means living with all our heart, passion, and dedication. We are consciously connected to our higher self and live heart-centered, aligned with our soul's purpose. We are making our destiny.

Success is defined as achieving what we have deliberately chosen as our purpose, goal, and mission. It gives our lives meaning, and we go for it with all our spirit.

When we connect with our true spirit and live our lives, heart first, we automatically start to do good and attract the good things in life. We begin to live generously with grace. Nothing in the heart can harm anything or anyone. There is no harm in the heart, and it can't do it. The heart can only follow a love-based agenda: joy fuels our soul.

Harm to ourselves, others, and the Earth is not an act of the heart; it's an act out of our distorted mind. When our mind is cluttered with dusty clouds, it follows a result-based agenda. Most of us are stuck in this without knowing it. We chase outside success, like more economic growth and power, but this is an unfulfilling path. The outside success can never fill the empty void. There are plenty of examples of that. Only when we have aligned with the deeper levels of the heart will we be fulfilled. Then, what we choose in the outside world will be a preference.

Richness is the feeling of being fulfilled, that we have enough, that we are enough.

As history tells us, harm can also be done by spiritual or religious leaders who think they act out of the heart but have become victims of dogma. There is a spiritual blindness in our world; we believe we are good or do good because we are spiritual because we go to church every Sunday or do yoga. It doesn't matter if we are spiritual; what matters is our level of consciousness. There is a higher consciousness and a more systemic way of living. Only when the human is whole and centered in its heart will the outside actions and manifestations fill the void.

To act on aggression and choose battle or fight is an example of a distorted mind.

Humans have fought other humans throughout history, even in the name of God or Jesus. Before the battle, our priests prayed to God to give us victory and protect us. God would probably answer, "Ok, but hey guys, the other side just asked me the same thing, so I will let you do whatever you think is a good idea and take good care of the souls you will waste with your lousy decision. But go ahead, it's your choice. I will not give victory to anyone who kills another. That's out of the question for me."

Some would argue that there are different sides to the coin and that we should try to see every side of the situation and not judge and that we should. Though the history and old, repeated patterns behind the situation do not justify the continuation of debate and conflict, the continuation of illusion and drama is not even in God's name. That only maintains old patterns and keeps us repeating history, playing the same record on repeat. Those who argue for this have forgotten or not yet understood that neither of the parties is right; humanity is only stuck in the drama, and there is a higher conscious way of living that goes beyond the current situation.

Take the old Israel and Palestine conflict as an example. Neither side says, "Ok, it's enough. Let's look at all of this from a distance. Let's let go of the past and unite here in peace, and we can live side by side if we choose to. No one has the right to the land; the land belongs to itself, to Mother Earth, and we are only visitors. So let's play along." But they don't because they do not want to or are too afraid to be defeated. Those who argue would say it's not that simple. The history is too long. But it would be straightforward if we could only let go.

God, Mohammed, or whoever we believe in has nothing to do with it and never has. The choice of battle is the act of a distorted mind, the will of power over, not power to. It's the act of the predator we all have inside, programmed by the harshness of living conditions through the ages. Someone came up with the idea that "If I kill the other gang, I can grab their food, and my family will survive." Since that seemed to work out, we've started to grow a lousy habit. Today, we do more or less the same but in a much more sophisticated way.

It was never the intention of Jesus or Mohammed that they should be worshipped or that we should use them as an excuse to kill someone else. That's just rubbish, but it's still not a part of our past. They are probably both sitting, looking at us, and saying, "We gave them our lives, but they still don't get it."

The ruthlessness of the distorted and result-based agenda has shown its face and keeps doing that. Living heart-centered in a world where unconscious ruthlessness outpowers the good is a gigantic challenge and, at the same time, so easy since the good will always win. History has shown that the fundamental life force is reasonable.

During the Congo Crisis, Dag Hammarskjöld's commitment to peace and diplomacy exemplified heart-centered leadership, even at the cost of his own life. Unfortunately, he fell victim to brutality in Congo in 1961 when his plane crashed. The reason behind the crash, whether it was shot down or not, is still hidden in the dark. He challenged ruthlessness with his peaceful mind and deliberate work to bring the world peace during his time as general secretary. During the Suez Crisis, he personally played a significant role, as he also did in the Congo Crisis. He had sat out on a mission to unite the nations that were not that united then, at the beginning of the Cold

War. He had a mindset and a heart-centered being, a way of being persistent in his beliefs, which was probably intriguing for those with another agenda. Though he died, his spirit lives on in the UN organization.

Our mind is made to be a toolbox for our hearts, not the opposite. Therefore, when we choose to live in spirit first, we choose the path of grace.

Let's use sports as an example. The drive to compete with others goes away when we live spirit-full, but we still want to succeed in what we have chosen to explore. We want to master the thing itself. The will to compete goes away because we understand that there is nothing such as competition; only others have chosen to do the same thing as we have, and they want to be good at it, too. So they have tuned in on the same thing.

If we live truly out of our hearts and race in a sport, we do not compete. Choosing wisely not to harm anyone on your course is good racing. If you cross the finish line first, it just means you have done your thing very well. We have done what we love, and we have done it with all our hearts. If we stand on the top of the podium, that's great. It was your day. If we don't, we salute those who stand there and align even stronger with our heart until next time, to where our decided heart takes us.

We might win the race if we act out of the energy to beat the others. Still, most of the time, we would only have our focus on beating them instead of doing our best. We will adapt to their level of performance, wasting our energy thinking of how we can beat them instead of what it would be like to be outstanding in my game. This is why we should focus on our success, not stop others from trying to achieve theirs. This does not mean we can't compare to others; the sound comparison is to know how to learn from others.

The grace in sports is called sportsmanship, and success is that we do what we love and love what we do, and we do it well because we choose to do it deliberately.

The power of the heart is tremendous; it overcomes anything, given the prerequisite that you are alive.

The heart center contains:

- Joy with the deeper level connected to the soul.
- Grief or sadness with the deeper level to a new beginning.
- Humbleness with a deeper level of softness.
- Hope with a deeper level of gratitude.
- Anger with the deeper level of transformation.
- Ego with a deeper level of compassion.
- Harmony with the deeper level of blessing.
- Sweetness with a deeper level of grace.
- Wisdom with a deeper level of sacred knowledge.

When we connect to the deeper levels of the heart, we can't do harm. That's why a spirit-full leader always knows to go to the heart before the mind, understanding that the mind is a toolbox for the heart to succeed in whatever we have chosen. When we stand at the center of our hearts, we embody love.

"A spirit-full leader inspires others to live with purpose, passion, and kindness."

~ Unknown

Being a Spirit-Full Leader in a Fast-Moving and Changing World

$$\longrightarrow\!\circ\!\mathcal{C}\!\!\sim\!\!\!\circ\!\circ\!\longrightarrow$$

I t's always easier to shut down, be narrow-minded, shrink our perspectives, be small, and let the ego take over than to stay open-minded and, in challenging times, expand our perspectives to move forward. Having the gift of doing so is the gift of the spirit-full leader. Just as leaders in the past had to navigate complex religious and geopolitical landscapes, today's leaders also have to confront the relentless tide of technology. In such a rapidly changing environment, the principles of spirit-full leadership become even more critical.

We have a fast-moving and exponentially changing world, which in many cases is very good, but like the old saying, "You shall not run faster than your soul can keep up." Unfortunately, far too often, our minds run faster into the future than our hearts, and we are unaware of it. So, let's briefly reflect on technology before heading on.

Only 100-150 years ago, even Kings and Queens could not do what almost everyone can do today. It was not even technologically possible. Imagine where we will be in 100 years.

My father used to say, "Every change is the biggest change of that time," and he is right. The biggest change is always the latest we experience. At the beginning of the 19th century, we had inventions like the telephone, the lightbulb, electricity, cars, and aviation. These were a rare luxury even for Kings and Queens. During the sixties, seventies, and eighties, there were the women's rights movement and the early days of the information age.

Just 15-20 years ago, we got smartphones, which have revolutionized how we communicate and shop. The market's largest companies are Amazon, Apple, Meta, and Tesla. The next era is that of artificial intelligence. So, we have a technological development that produces a rapid evolution in consumption—a technological development that shakes humanity to the bone, and the speed of consumption globally that just 150 years ago was not even thought of.

Just as leaders in the past had to navigate complex religious and geopolitical landscapes, today's leaders confront the relentless tide of technology. In such a rapidly changing environment, the principles of spirit-full leadership become even more critical.

Technological development is progressing exponentially, faster than our souls can run. However, when used for the good of humankind, it can greatly advance the world. This places a heightened demand on leadership. To not fall into the traps of the past patterns, it's easy to be blinded by the speed, to be narrowed-sighted only to look at the result-based agenda. It's comparable to driving at high speeds; your field of vision narrows. Maneuvering at such velocities requires exceptional skills, peripheral vision, and a comprehensive perspective. Very few people possess these abilities, especially in everyday life. To truly understand speed means having control over space and time. Those who have experienced it understand that everything seems to move slowly, giving the feeling of plenty of time to react.

The current world's evolution and technological development demand increased awareness, presence, and consciousness from leaders. Skills that cannot be studied in the ways we are used to, at universities or by reading books. Instead, skills need to be explored, trained, practiced, and discovered through meditation, stillness, frequency guidance, and a focus that springs from a deeply centered being.

Not only has technology developed over the last 100 years, but civil rights, women's rights, school systems, healthcare, welfare, medicine, and many other areas have also seen significant improvements worldwide.

We would never like to go back, and why should we? Evolution will never go backward; it always goes forward. The universe only goes forward, and it expands; it's now. So, we cannot go back to living as we did in the past centuries. We will inevitably move forward. While we might reduce our travel or reliance on certain technologies momentarily, the path ahead is paved with new innovations. The goal is to transition to a more sustainable way of living, drawing lessons from the past. Although there might be brief periods of regression, the long-term perspective points towards progress and not reverting entirely.

In this rapidly changing world, the spirit-full leader has a huge role in enhancing and utilizing humanity's ancient and future wisdom into sacred universal knowledge. Remember, just 100 years ago, the technology was lightyears from what we have today. We can only look into the future to see what to create of it, and most things have not been invented yet.

Why is the spirit-full leader so crucial in this evolution? Because they are present and aware.

Some years ago, I led a 100-year workshop for a major city in a development process. We asked some historians to present to us what had happened in the region during the past 100 years and what political decisions had been made that had affected the present situation. We also thoroughly analyzed the present change patterns and gathered facts about the current situation. For the workshop, we gathered people from different professions. We gathered politicians, engineers, opera singers, artists, doctors, carpenters, priests, and other people with other skills for the workshop to get a representative part of the population together. The seminar's subject was what the world would look like 100 years from now and what it would be like in our local society.

After one day of the workshop, the most significant finding was not the idea of the future. The most significant result was that we are not conscious enough to let go of our present and past values to look into the future free of our current thinking of what life should and can be like. The group was not even aware that they were thinking that way. A way that is more common than we might think. When the group came to this insight, there became a silence in the room, where people started to contemplate what they had just experienced.

That's why the spirit-full leader is so essential for our evolution. They are concerned about evolving, knowing their responsibility, and being aware and present. They know their greatest legacy is their personal growth and what it will contribute to the world. A leader that is fully connected to the heart, can feel the good energies at play deep inside, no matter what the turbulence outside is about.

"The leadership spirit possesses a natural love for all human beings."

~ Myles Munroe

Aligned with Purpose

One thing that characterizes spirit-full leaders is that they seem to have a strong why, a deep connection to their soul's purpose; they understand why they are here. Many of them seem to be so-called seekers or, as I would like to express it, explorers. Seekers or explorers, the finders of truth. What's really true?

To be a seeker has, in many religions or societies, been a way to say that someone is lost, has not found their purpose, or is not of true faith, especially in extremely secular societies. But I think it's the opposite; the seeker or explorer has a calling to set out into the adventure of the great mystery. A calling they might not even be consciously aware of. Many of them also feel a lot of doubt and uncertainty.

When transformation into spirit-full leadership occurs through increased awareness and maturation, some wisdom enters the void, the empty space created through expansion. There is more room for knowledge to take superiority over the ego and the need to fill the void with more consumption, economic growth, and willpower.

There is no superiority in knowing your why with your mind, with words. It only makes it easier to share it with others if we do. There is a greater knowing where we know our purpose, sense it, and are guided by it without words.

The greater knowing is not based on knowledge; the closest description is intuition, the knowing without knowing. We do not think; we know it's not a gut feeling either; gut feelings can fool us.

The knowing we talk about is something greater, and it's beyond the feeling, the thoughts, and the mind.

The why we talk about here is also something greater than what we can think or express with words quite far from the superficial management platitudes we can see in most companies. It's a calling, something that you can't resist, and you must follow it; you must go that way. If you resist, you will be called repeatedly until you obey the calling.

It's a purpose that pulls in a certain direction, even if it's not apparent what the focus or goal is.

Innocence

The spirit-full leader has grown or is growing an expression of innocence. You can see it in the person's eyes and acts, just in their presence. It expresses a deeper understanding of life, and their aura gets a certain glow to it.

This is the innocence of a child, but it is not childish. Instead, it's an innocence that unfolds from a life lived to the fullest, an experience that has matured into wisdom and an acceptance of life and its endless wonders. Innocence grows by expanding the heart center, increasing compassion, and understanding our path.

When we awaken and start to ascend to a greater understanding of life and the great mystery, we become more and more innocent in practice. The process is that we become increasingly aware of our illusions, false identities, masks, shadows, and illusions of society. And we accept them in our hearts to the level that they lose their grip on us. We let go of them, and they don't affect or infect us as much anymore.

The result is that the childlike amusement and joy of even the smallest things becomes significant. The innocent child often wants to pick the beautiful flower, and the childish innocence intends to have it. But the innocent leader sees the flower, gets amazed by it, wants to see it grow, gives support, and fertilizes the soil to grow just because it's possible.

The innocent leader does not consider themselves a leader and does not want anything from the other. He only wants to share his wisdom and co-create a healthy and sound reality. Knowing that everything else is just an illusion.

Without him being a real person, just a character, Superman is an excellent example of this. He has superpowers, but still, he chooses to use them for the greater good, not only for his benefit, like his nemesis Lex Luthor. Or he uses them to save his immense love, Lois. Sometimes, he lives like Clark Kent and amuses himself by flying around just because he can. You can see the innocence in his melancholic-loving eyes.

The innocence we discuss here is a superpower, especially as a leader, if we can develop it.

Some people who show this are Mother Theresa, Nelson Mandela, Dag Hammarskjöld, and Gandhi. They had magnificence in their eyes, and they emitted peace. Two of them were also awarded a Nobel Peace Prize for their contribution. All of them were truly dedicated to their mission, gave it all, and gave up many things most people would never give up. Although they were not average, they were like anyone in their humbleness. They did not put themselves on a pedestal, saying they knew everything.

In a simpler and more earthbound way, we could say that we develop this when our ego starts to lose its grip on us, when we get out of the narcosis and have a clearer view, or when we have seen and experienced so much that we know our insignificance to the extent that we are amused by just existing, just flying around because we can.

We take ourselves seriously unserious and do not have to be a world leader to reach this state, probably the opposite. This could also be the fisherman, who knows his life purpose, the woman who runs the gas station, or the teacher whose ego does not need to teach. He does it with all his heart.

A colleague used to say, "There is a lack of love" in our business, and he is correct: there is a lack of love. It's the power of love that makes innocence. It's the love of power that makes the opposite.

Following the love-based agenda brings innocence, and being a servant of greater values makes us humble.

An essential step in growing profound innocence is to make up for death, to die from our beliefs and illusions so we can start to live fully. To realize that we are actually equal before death and cannot bring anything with us when we die, not even our status. We might be remembered, but to what good is that for us? Of course, it might benefit our relatives to say, I'm the son or relative of Mr. X, or get a big inheritance, but that does not make you a good person, a good leader, or give you any higher value. It might give you benefits in life, but it will not give you any help when you die. In the moment of death, we are all the same. The spirit leaves the body, and the light is switched off. We won't remember our funeral; we can't smell the flowers on the altar or hear the beautiful words that people we leave say about us.

It doesn't matter if you are famous or unknown; the micro-moment of death is the same. Most people avoid death as a subject; otherwise, it is preferable. How could we live by that innocent joy if we do not accept death? Accepting death is accepting life. It is not something to wander around thinking of all day or try to work on, but when the moment comes out of realization, a new level of innocence enters.

Accepting death can come in many shapes. Personally, it came from two radical motorcycle accidents with near-death experiences. After that, I've spent a lot of energy working on healing the trauma. I could have died, but I am living. Then, becoming a father of two beautiful daughters depends on you for a long time, and you are a living person, not the walking dead. So, that has affected me on every level, especially as a leader and a father, which is also a leadership role.

Innocence is not about being naive; it's about being extremely present, being one with existence, knowing your insignificance, and, by that, acknowledging your greatness.

The innocent leader is not scheming or manipulative. He does not try to figure out how to control or drive something in a specific direction. He is not trying to usurp benefits for himself. He is instead greatly rewarded for his achievements as a person just by being.

Connected

Being a spirit-full leader is effortless. It's an integrated part of your being and comes easily and naturally. It's based on a cultivated connection with yourself and your higher self.

I believe there is a reason that specific persons end up in particular positions and act in an exact way. That reason is the person being connected or disconnected.

Let's take the world's greatest living spiritual and awakened leader on the one hand and, on the other hand, the mega-billionaire corporate leader. Would the spiritual leader consciously be able to do what the corporate leader does? The answer is no. It would be going against his conscious connection to his higher self. Let's take another example: two presidents taking on the role of president for the same nation in very different ways. One tells many stories, even lies, and the other tries to bring in a welfare system to make it better for a whole nation, using entirely different ways of acting. Or the person who believes that more guns make it a safer place.

The author, Brené Brown, has defined connection comprehensively and brilliantly:

"The energy that exists between people when they feel seen, heard, and valued; when they can give and receive without judgment; and when they derive sustenance and strength from the relationship."

Since we are in relation with everything and everyone on some level, I believe this is also an excellent explanation of a connected person's relationship with his self and higher self, also known as source, love, God, or the life force Qi. Without a conscious connection to the life force, it's impossible to have a connected relationship. This internal relation in an awakened state may make some people act more consciously than others.

Staying connected in our world can be a tremendous challenge. For example, we could be challenged with situations where we are attacked and must fight for our lives, or we can't flee a dreadful situation. In these situations, the human mechanism is to disconnect to be able to do the things we need to survive. However, for most people and leaders, this is a rare situation; still, we continuously disconnect and stay disconnected in everyday life. The reason is that our old brains, memories, and programming can't separate between being attacked by a mountain lion and being attacked by opponents in a debate or around the dinner table. In both situations, we either will be playing dead to avoid being harmed, or we will start to fight for our survival. Maybe we disconnect and lose our sense of perspective, our humanness, and stay in that disconnected state for years, causing all kinds of illness and distortion in our lives and the lives of others.

Though we can reconnect at any time, we may need some help to do it and remember how it feels. The leaders we see as role models in this book are connected and centered, which means they are solid under pressure. They are grounded and have deep roots firmly fixed into the soil. They have integrity and a connection to nature. They do not harm or abuse anyone or anything. Their mind will stay clear, resting in their heart.

A friend said, "There is a need for a medicine man in every board room." Medicine is also known as love in ancient wisdom. By this, he means a person with knowledge and someone who takes in a greater perspective, has the gift to heal and takes responsibility for more than the financial result and the dividend. That knows future generations might need to pay the mortgage cost for the profit we make now.

At the top, we are at the helm in both the upwind and the tailwind, and many times, we want reality to work for us to achieve goals, longings, and dreams. As leaders, we need to act to create the future situation, and it's not enough only to react to what's given. And we usually put in a lot of effort to make it happen, or else we would not have been the top leaders. In practice, this means navigating the strategic challenge to lead daily operations, lead change, develop business, and change habits and thought patterns simultaneously until we align with what we set out to be!

"When people do things together, it will have effects and consequences. Do they lead us to reach what we want, or do they lead to something else?"
– Hans E Annonsen

As mentioned before, we can only lead or change ourselves, which means how we think, act, operate, and relate to everything and everyone around us. The manager is a position in which we are given a certain power level. A leader is something others make us when they choose to follow. Finding a balance between the two is key! When we act and operate, reality will respond by either working for us or challenging us with things we have, consciously or unconsciously, chosen to learn from. This equals both the leader and the follower.

The ability to navigate this beautiful chaos inside and out is what unfolds potential; that's how we innovate ourselves. When we cultivate connectedness, we, step by step, become self-contained but not self-absorbed. The self-contained individual finds joy in mutual co-dependence without relying on external validation.

Great leaders usually have a calling, commitment, determination, and the will to succeed. If or when that commitment is turned inwards to the connectedness, it's all that is needed. Being connected comes with higher levels of consciousness, more understanding, and greater perspectives. This turns into more humanness, completeness, and awareness of who we are and what we do, and the empty void will not be open but be filled with love.

Sustainable

Spirit-full leaders are sustainable in themselves, their manners, and their decisions regarding treating others and using resources. They are not without flaws, quite the opposite. They know their weaknesses and do not try to justify them by explanation.

Sustainability is the awareness that there is no planet B, no second Earth, and neither is there a B version of you or me. It is also an expression of the realization that you are another me. The ancient Hermetic phrase "As above, so below; as within, so without" suggests that the micro reflects the macro, and our internal states mirror the external. In the context of sustainability, this means our personal habits and attitudes reflect on a larger scale in our surroundings and the planet.

To understand the subject of sustainability, we first should look inside at ourselves. How sustainable are we with ourselves? Do we live sustainably with our resources? What energy do we operate from? What feelings do we emit? What thoughts do we think? What do we project on others? What words come out of our mouths?

We seem to think we can compensate for our behaviors and decisions by buying ourselves things that make us feel responsibility-free. We give charity money and buy clothes manufactured at meager wages or compensate for our weekend flight by buying emission rights. Unfortunately, we can't accept ourselves as free; the only way to do this is to look at our footprint. If it leaves more than a fresh scent of grace after us, we have a bit to go.

The truth is that we are energy, and we are each other's environment. We all infect, transmit, and absorb energy and viruses from each other. However, mature leaders have control of their energy and choose wisely what they send out and take in. Another truth, in this case, is that we are not responsible for anyone else's energy. We are responsible for ourselves and what we bring to the situation and leave behind.

If we want a non-toxic, non-polluted environment and a world of equality, we should strive to be non-toxic and equal. When we become aware of this, we long for a cleaner life, to be cleaner in ourselves, and to feed ourselves with more high-frequency food, circumstances, and people. To be or start to long for or appeal to a non-toxic or clean way of living is an effect of awakening. When our vibration ascends, our body yearns for fresh everything. Drugs, alcohol, meat, smoking, porn, abuse, crime, greed, discrimination, and overconsumption are all part of toxic energies.

I am not a saint in any way, but that does not make it less true. It only says that I have not been able to live according to what I have understood yet, so I have not understood it fully because if I had, I would have acted following my understanding. It is a universal truth that we understand what we know and act in accordance with our present knowledge.

When I share this in my coaching, leadership, or management consulting, I sometimes get laughter or comments that I am dull or too severe, and that would make life boring. There must be a little party, and I should loosen up and have more fun. But happiness is not about parties, and it's not about spraying champagne, even though it's fun. It's a frequency that can be experienced by anyone regardless of outer circumstances, though it's easier in some cases than others. When we have shared this for a while, we usually end up in the crank reality of realization, and it becomes quiet, and after a time, real peace enters the room, the peace that lays the foundation for happiness. The spirit-full leadership is not to avoid unpleasant feelings and realizations, and it's to face ourselves and the situation in its truth. Bringing out real harmony, happiness, and sustainability, not fake. To create a non-toxic environment where we can thrive.

Spirit-full leaders are sustainable at heart, aware of the balance, and we are always ascending or descending, and there is always a movement. Energy is constantly moving, decomposing, or manifesting; in this movement, they know how to bring harmony to the situation and use resources wisely. This does not mean they live like ascetics; they know the consequences of who they are and how they choose.

An example of awareness is balancing electricity use by refraining from googling everything. In the last 20 years, the digital revolution has exponentially increased. Most people today take that for granted, just like switching on the light when we enter a room. What not everyone thinks of when we are posting or looking at social media or googling our questions is that all this is powered by gigantic computer sites worldwide, which consume gigantic amounts of electricity to cool servers to keep them running. For now, the amount of electricity we use is such that alternative electric productions can't suffice the need. I do not mean we should stop evolution, but we can be more aware of our actions. If each of us could reduce our use of digital solutions by as little as one percent, that would save a huge amount of electricity.

"Leadership is not about taking charge, leadership is about taking care of those in our charge."

~ Simon Sinek

Leadership and Performance

O ften, when the subject of leadership comes up in a conversation, I have noticed that people stiffen, lose their softness, get anxious, and are not comfortable anymore. The conversation often becomes a little edgy and complicated instead of joyful and curious. I have many times wondered why. My theory is that the subject of leadership, throughout history, has been imprinted with a lot of false illusions and delusions that leadership is about supervising, command, control, manipulation, performance, results, demands, and getting people to do things they do not want, using power to control people or just someone we have to obey. And it has been that way for ages. Nothing can be more wrong because that's not leadership, something else, or misusing the power in a position.

Leadership is something else, just as we have talked about. It's about inspiring and influencing people so they make you a leader, hopefully, with excellent, honest intentions.

The new leadership paradigm contains many more spirit-full values, which we address in this book. The new leadership paradigm balances the inside fulfillment and the outside manifestation of feminine and masculine aspects. What will the true words to this new paradigm of leadership be? We don't know, but we have an idea.

It's impossible to talk about leadership without talking about performance. There is always a sense of performance in any subject and situation, even for the spiritual masters, just as the responsibility. The word performance is often connected with results, but performance is actually in its purer meaning, being there and showing up for yourself to be the best version of yourself.. Preferably measured inside and out, remember the definition of success.

Let's take a business leader, for example. If you want to sell your goods or service more than once, if you're going to sell repeatedly more than anything, the energy you emit in the whole process, from idea to delivery, is important. Your energy level is imprinted on everything, and everyone involved during this process. Consider Apple. Steve Jobs, a leader known for his relentless focus on product quality, imbued a certain energy into Apple products. This energy, or essence, can be felt when you use an Apple device, and it's a big part of why the brand has such a loyal following. We can always sell something once, but to multiply and sell to the same customer and repeatedly perform, there needs to be a certain quality involved. That quality is the energy level you emit and put into the process. In this process, everyone is a leader.

The chef Gordon Ramsey's methods and way of expressing himself might seem harsh, but it's an example of the above. You will feel it if a restaurant does not cook with love, and you would probably never return. However, Gordon's tough love coaching helps restaurants in need to unfold their potential. Even though it's a TV show, it's an excellent example of what happens when a group of people make a tiny change in awareness. They get a little more in contact with the soul of cooking, and their energies start to move in a new direction, resulting in the food's taste, the service being better, and the customers returning. It does not matter if you are a Michelin-star restaurant or a food truck on the street; the same laws are at play. A Michelin-star restaurant can live quite long on the reputation it had acquired from once having a star even if its food is not at star level anymore, but the food truck never can.

Knowing that energy always comes first, then comes matter, it's how you build a brand. You cannot talk about being green and sustainable and then throw a plastic bottle into the ocean. It's not aligned. That's the cross purpose of energies. And truth, the good, will always show itself, sooner or later.

As a leader, you might influence and inspire your peers to change or do something once. However, doing it repeatedly and perhaps evolving to new levels of humanity demands more than an intelligent selling pitch. We need to become the energy we want to realize and live the reality we want to have.

This is a hard fact for most of us, but nevertheless, it's true. The law of attraction is inevitable, like attracts like. Try, and you will notice.
If we want creativity – be creative.
If we want trust – be trustworthy.
If we want sustainability – be sustainable.
If we want love – be loving.
And it continues.

So, reframing performance into showing up to be the best version of me has given me a completely new way of seeing the performance, showing up as the person and reality we want to see manifested, and being that wholehearted. Then, the spirit-full leader embodies the qualities they want to see in the world, being role models. This reframes leadership and performance.

"I think leadership is service and there is power in that giving: to help people, to inspire and motivate them to reach their fullest potential."

~ Denise Morrison

Exploring Spirit-Full Leaders

To deepen our understanding of what spirit-full means, it is necessary to define its two main components: *spirit-full* and *leader*. The word *spirit* refers to what most people consider the life force or animating force inside living things. Therefore, the spirit refers to the utmost importance of the relationship with the self and the environment.

The word *leader* generally refers to a person who holds a prominent position of authority or influence and is responsible for guiding, directing, and motivating a group or organization toward a common goal.

A spirit-full leader shows the way by going in front with compassion and leading others to follow a course of action or line of thinking. Therefore, a spirit-full leader affects the beliefs and actions of those they lead.

When taken together, the two concepts indicate that a leader who incorporates spirituality into their leadership inspires their followers to learn more about themselves on a deep, personal level and give their lives meaning. One way to describe spirituality in leadership is as a whole-person approach in which the leader tries to give people a sense of drive and connection.

- Using moral and ethical standards from a holistic point of view is a sign of spirit-full leadership. The spirit-full leader cares about the whole person, not just the employee, and this helps people find purpose in their lives. By promoting a positive work culture that values collaboration and growth, spirit-full leaders create an environment where employees or the community feel valued and supported. They also celebrate achievements, encourage open communication, and genuinely care for their team members' well-being. Through these actions, spirit-full leaders enable their followers to connect emotionally to their work, fostering a greater sense of fulfillment and meaning in their job.

I remember one of my first leadership roles after I sold my landscaping business. It was for an American personal development company based in Ubud, Bali. I was the head of sales and generally led from the front, challenging the team to keep up with my call output. I was disciplined, expecting everyone to at least be on time, if not early, for the day ahead. Because a large portion of our client base was in the US and the UK, it wasn't uncommon for me to schedule calls late at night or in the early hours of the morning.

This was back at the beginning of 2013, when I was in the infant stages of developing my spiritual practice, relying on tough love to motivate my team, often taking the spotlight. I was afraid that if I gave the spotlight to individuals on my team, they might take my position. We were doing well, but we could have been so much better. The owner of the company encouraged me to elevate my team instead of competing with them. Once I began noticing the strengths of the individuals on my team, even the person who desired my position, our sales collectively improved. My insecurities dissipated when I stopped competing and began empathizing with my team members.

I've learned that being a spirit-full leader calls for a person with high introspection, who listens to advice, and who is humble. Self-awareness is necessary for any spirit-full leader who wants to guide their team in a non-traditional, self-assured, and caring way.

Spirit-full leaders need to take stock of their strengths and weaknesses, hopes, aspirations, and the demands of the global community. The leader's idea gives the team a reason to work together, motivates them to do so, and shows their culture. Just as important is the spirit-full leader's ability to communicate this vision, which encourages followers to work together, bringing the idea to life.

As Stefan and I have discussed earlier, self-awareness is one of the top values of every spirit-full leader, aiding them to develop and articulate an inspiring vision. They must go on inside and learn to live with their brightness and darkness. To keep from putting their weaknesses, fears, limits, pains, and insecurities onto other people, they need to first accept and acknowledge these things about themselves. This kind of value ultimately results in a more fulfilling life.

Spirit-full leaders value authenticity and lead by example, staying true to their beliefs, principles, and values. They are transparent in their actions and decisions, earning the trust and respect of their team by being genuine and honest. They know the factors influencing their decision-making and where their strengths and weaknesses lie. They can see patterns in themselves that might cloud their judgment and make it hard to make good decisions. Wise leaders are those who are willing to put their egos aside and listen to the advice of others around them. They encourage people to share their skills and ideas and value the contributions of others. Moreover, they have enough confidence in themselves to allow others to thrive.

Empathy is a cornerstone of spirit-full leadership. Knowing that we are ultimately all one actively listening to our team members is easy, along with understanding different perspectives and showing genuine care for the well-being of the tribe or community. Spirit-full leaders create a supportive and compassionate work environment by empathizing with others. This forms the foundation for building meaningful connections with team members and fostering a positive culture. Showing empathy allows spirit-full leaders to create an environment that nurtures emotional well-being, fosters collaboration, and builds strong relationships with their team. By leading with empathy, these leaders inspire trust, loyalty, and dedication in their employees or whoever they guide.

Spirit-full leaders value diversity and inclusivity within the organization. They embrace different perspectives, backgrounds, and experiences, fostering an inclusive environment where everyone feels valued and heard. Spirit-full leaders enrich their teams by promoting diversity with various ideas and solutions. The goal of the spirit-full leader is to create an environment where individuals of similar faiths and values may work together harmoniously.

As mentioned earlier, spirit-full leaders possess a clear and inspiring vision of the future. They communicate this vision effectively, motivating their team toward common goals. Their compelling vision helps people find meaning and purpose in their work. A clear vision is a top value for spirit-full leaders because it is a guiding light that inspires and motivates their team members. It creates a cohesive and motivated collective, attracting top talent and driving the vision toward success and a positive impact on humanity.

Spirit-full leaders prioritize the needs of their team and serve as mentors, coaches, and supporters. They focus on empowering their team members and helping them grow personally and professionally. Servant leadership is a top value for spirit-full leaders because it encapsulates the essence of leading with empathy, compassion, and a focus on serving others. It complements the spirit-full leadership approach by emphasizing the well-being and growth of team members. Servant leadership contributes to higher levels of employee engagement. When team members feel valued and supported, they are more motivated and committed.

When you lead from a spiritual point of view, you shift your focus from formal positional authority to the people under it, from an emphasis on conformity to a focus on change and variety, and from command and control to partnership, cooperation, and inspiration. A spiritually enlightened way of leading doesn't require religious belief or trying to change people's minds.

Leaders who emphasize spirituality can get their ideas for how to lead from different religious traditions, but they can also be atheists or have non-traditional religious views. Spirit-full leadership helps people become well-rounded people who care about their coworkers, managers, customers, and the community.

Spiritual leaders are also defined by honesty, benevolence, and genuine concern for others. Now to dive deeper into the values of great spirit-full leaders of the last century:

One of the most famous examples of a spirit-full leader who took an organization from disarray to productive harmony using spiritual techniques is Mahatma Gandhi and his role in leading the Indian independence movement against British colonial rule.

In the early 20th century, India faced widespread disarray due to British oppression, economic hardship, and political division. Thus, Mahatma Gandhi emerged as a spirit-full leader, inspiring the masses through his nonviolent approach and deeply spiritual principles.

Vision and Purpose: Gandhi aimed to achieve India's independence through nonviolent civil disobedience. He communicated this vision effectively, uniting people from diverse backgrounds and inspiring them to join the freedom movement.

- **Servant Leadership:** Gandhi epitomized servant leadership, placing the interests of the Indian people before his own. He lived a simple life, identifying with the poor and marginalized, and consistently advocated for their rights and welfare.

- **Nonviolence and Compassion:** Gandhi's core principle was Ahimsa (nonviolence) and compassion toward all living beings. He believed in the power of love and kindness even in the face of brutal repression from the British authorities.

- **Inclusivity and Unity:** Gandhi emphasized unity and inclusivity, bringing together people from various religions, castes, and regions of India. He rejected divisive practices and advocated for unity among Indians against colonial rule.

- **Empathy and Understanding:** Gandhi empathized with the plight of the Indian population. He traveled extensively across the country, understanding their challenges and inspiring them to be self-reliant.

- **Moral Leadership:** Gandhi led by moral example, emphasizing the importance of truth, honesty, and integrity. He encouraged people to be truthful, even in the face of adversity, gaining immense trust and respect from his followers.

- **Mass Mobilization and Satyagraha:** Gandhi employed the principle of *Satyagraha*, which means truth force or soul force. Through nonviolent resistance and civil disobedience, he mobilized millions of Indians to participate in protests, boycotts, and strikes.

- **Spiritual Fasting:** On several occasions, Gandhi used spiritual fasting as a protest to bring unity and harmony among conflicting parties. His fasts were powerful tools for reconciliation and negotiation.

Through Gandhi's spiritual techniques, India's freedom movement gained immense momentum. His actions and values inspired millions to rise above differences and work together toward a common goal. The result was a productive harmony transcending caste, religion, and regional divisions.

Gandhi's spirit-full leadership was crucial to India's eventual independence in 1947. His legacy continues to inspire individuals and movements worldwide.

Empathy

Nelson Mandela states, "People must learn to hate, and if they can learn to hate, they can be taught to love, for love comes more naturally to the human heart than its opposite."

Selflessness and affection are inseparable. Unconditional love requires altruism; likewise, philanthropy cannot be defined apart from unconditional love. True love is sometimes compared to the unconditional love shared by family members, members of the same military unit, or partners in a long-term, committed relationship.

There is no stronger feeling than love, which is why its antitheses, such as hatred and apathy, are so destructive. It is the most potent and mysterious phenomenon in our society, yet it reveals itself as straightforward and available to anybody when actively sought. One of the signs that I love someone is when their well-being and safety matter to me as much as or more than my own. This is the state of mind that results from loving someone so passionately that one prioritizes that person's pleasure over one's own.

In the face of racial segregation, discrimination, and deep-rooted hatred, Martin Luther King Jr. emerged as a powerful advocate for civil rights and social justice. He led the nonviolent civil rights movement, promoting equality and racial harmony.

- **Unconditional Love and Nonviolence:** Martin Luther King Jr. believed in the power of unconditional love and nonviolence. He was deeply influenced by the teachings of Mahatma Gandhi and adopted the principle of nonviolent resistance to fight for justice.

- **A Vision of Equality:** King had a powerful vision of a united America where people of all races could live together in harmony and equality. He dreamt of a future where people would be judged by their character's content, not their skin color.

- **Empathy and Understanding:** King empathized with the struggles of the black American community. He understood their pain and suffering, and his compassion fueled his determination to fight for their rights and dignity.

- **Moral and Spiritual Leadership:** King led by moral example, consistently preaching the message of love, forgiveness, and compassion. He infused his speeches with spiritual wisdom, appealing to the nation's moral conscience.

- **Inclusivity and Unity:** King emphasized inclusivity and unity, advocating for people from all walks of life to join the civil rights movement. He sought to bridge the racial divide and build coalitions with individuals and organizations committed to the cause of justice.

- **Turning the Other Cheek:** In the face of violent opposition and hate, King maintained a stance of turning the other cheek. He encouraged his followers not to respond to violence with violence but to respond with love and compassion.

- **Courage and Resilience:** King faced numerous challenges, including imprisonment, threats, and physical attacks, but he remained steadfast in his commitment to nonviolence and unconditional love. His courage and resilience inspired others to stand up for their rights.

- **Love for All Humanity:** King's vision of unconditional love extended beyond race; it encompassed all of humanity. He believed love was the most potent force for transforming hearts and society.

Martin Luther King Jr.'s spirit-full leadership, guided by unconditional love and nonviolence, was pivotal in the Civil Rights Movement. His powerful speeches, peaceful protests, and unwavering commitment to love and justice transformed the landscape of American society and paved the way for significant advancements in civil rights legislation. His legacy inspires generations to work toward a more just, loving, and inclusive world.

The highest human emotion, altruism, springs from a place of love. Those who love are not afraid to speak out when they see wrongdoing, and their examples remind us that we don't have to be consistently pleasant to be kind. Those who have lived selflessly leave an imprint on the world even after death. Their unselfish actions serve as examples for people who have lost faith in humanity and the status of the world. They are the metaphorical straws that drowning men cling to.

It was an ideology put into reality by historical figures, including Mahatma Gandhi, Yasmin Mogahed, Nelson Mandela, and Maya Angelou. Their devotion to all life forms served as a means to an end: developing into role models of genuine and courageous leaders. Many people like to talk about love and say nice things, but what matters is how you act on those words. The most elegant words will amount to nothing if they are not implemented.

Spirit-full leaders who lead with unconditional love can inspire positive change in their organizations and communities. Their approach encourages others to follow suit and adopt more compassionate and empathetic leadership styles. Instead of seeking to blame or punish, they focus on finding solutions that benefit everyone involved. Unconditional love nurtures positive relationships, empowers employees, and inspires commitment and loyalty, ultimately leading to the organization's and its people's growth and success.

Humility

One of the most famous examples of a spirit-full leader who led with humility is Nelson Mandela, the former President of South Africa and a key figure in the anti-apartheid movement.

In the 1990s, South Africa was grappling with the legacy of apartheid, a system of racial segregation and discrimination that had oppressed the majority black population for decades. When Nelson Mandela was released from prison in 1990 after 27 years of incarceration for his anti-apartheid activism, he had every reason to feel resentful and seek revenge. However, Mandela chose a different path – one of humility and reconciliation.

Throughout his life, Mandela demonstrated extraordinary humility, even as he became a global symbol of resistance and hope for the oppressed. Shortly after his release from prison, Mandela visited a small rural village in South Africa. As he walked through the town, the residents gathered around him, eager to hear him speak. Instead of delivering a grand speech or basking in the crowd's adulation, Mandela sat down with the villagers, listening to their stories, concerns, and aspirations.

He engaged with the people, asking questions and showing genuine interest in their lives. He recognized that he was just one part of a larger justice movement and humbly acknowledged the sacrifices and contributions of countless individuals who had fought for freedom alongside him.

During his presidency, Mandela continued to lead with humility, emphasizing the importance of unity and forgiveness. He invited leaders of the former apartheid regime to join his government, seeking to build a multiracial and inclusive nation. He acknowledged the pain of the past while advocating for reconciliation and healing.

Mandela's humility allowed him to connect with people from all walks of life. He saw himself as a servant of the people, not a ruler or a conqueror. He often said that he was not a saint but a person who made mistakes and learned from them. This honesty and humility endeared him to the nation and the world.

His spirit-full leadership, alongside with his humility, not only paved the way for a peaceful transition to democracy in South Africa but also left a lasting legacy of forgiveness, unity, and compassion. Mandela's ability to lead with humility, empathy, and a commitment to justice has inspired leaders worldwide to embrace humility as a powerful tool for transformational leadership. His story continues to resonate, reminding us of the profound impact that humble leaders can have on their people and the world.

Nelson Mandela was a man of strong spirit and determination. Though he battled fiercely for his ideals, he retained his humanity and humility throughout the ordeal. He said, "Don't back down from your convictions, but don't make an example of the opponents, either." When someone is made to feel ashamed, they become much more dangerous. To achieve peace, Mandela knew it was necessary to cooperate with and respect one's adversaries. This is where he showed us the value of teamwork and compromise.

A strong, spirit-full leader can debate openly and exhaustively, knowing that he and the opposing side will become closer and more united. You don't think that way when you're arrogant, superficial, and ignorant. The Nobel Peace Prize was shared by Nelson Mandela and the final head of South Africa's apartheid regime, FW de Klerk, in 1993. The two leaders symbolized cooperation and compromise to end apartheid peacefully and set the groundwork for a future democratic South Africa. Nelson Mandela summed up the events perfectly, saying, "Many seemingly intractable issues may be solved by the labor of a small, committed group of leaders who approach the subject objectively and have no personal stake in the result with a humble spirit."

A moral giant and a symbol of peace and forgiveness across the world, as described by Desmond Tutu, Nelson Mandela has inspired countless people. Mandela showed us that change is possible even when it seems impossible as long as courageous leaders band together, question the unquestioned, and challenge the status quo.

Imagine if there were more people like Nelson Mandela. Within your own company?

Within the context of your own family?

Humble, spirit-full leaders know exactly where they excel and where they fall short. They don't have any false notions about their abilities. Confidence and modesty may coexist. Generating confidence in one's talents and skills is a hallmark of a humble leader.

Leaders who embrace humility become better people, which you should do if you care about your followers. However, embracing modesty can benefit you in more ways than one. Additionally, those who practice humility tend to have more developed listening and empathic abilities.

- You'll improve as a leader when you learn to appreciate humility.

- If anything, you may improve as a person.

- All parties involved would benefit from that.

Humble leaders do more than merely allow their people to learn from missteps. In addition, they are self-aware, know that mistakes are within their capabilities, and are humble enough to accept blame when they make one.

A humble spirit-full leader can take many forms, depending on the individual. The fundamental idea is that even a leader may be brought down and you, like every other individual, have room for development.

Servant Leadership

One of the most famous examples of a spirit-full leader who embodied servant leadership is Mother Teresa, the Catholic nun and humanitarian known for her work with the poor and sick in Kolkata, India.

In the 1950s, Kolkata was rife with poverty, disease, and social inequality. Mother Teresa felt a strong calling to serve society's most marginalized and forgotten members. She founded the Missionaries of Charity in 1950, an organization dedicated to caring for the poorest of the poor.

In the heart of Kolkata's slums, a young girl was abandoned and left to fend for herself. She was malnourished, sick, and had lost all hope. Mother Teresa and her sisters came across the girl and immediately took her into their care.

Mother Teresa tended to the girl's wounds and provided her with food and medicine. She held the girl's hand, providing comfort and love as she began healing physically and emotionally. The young girl smiled again, finding a sense of belonging and love in Mother Teresa's presence.

As the girl's health improved, Mother Teresa arranged for her to attend school and receive an education. She nurtured the girl's potential, allowing her to learn and grow.

Throughout her life, Mother Teresa demonstrated an unwavering dedication to serving others. She embraced the principles of servant leadership, putting the needs of the poor and suffering above her own. She lived a simple and humble life, wearing a plain sari and walking the same streets as those she served.

Mother Teresa's spirit-full servant leadership extended beyond her immediate care for individuals. She inspired a global movement of volunteers and missionaries who followed her example of selfless service to humanity. Her work reached far beyond Kolkata, as the Missionaries of Charity established homes and missions around the world, caring for the destitute, sick, and dying.

Mother Teresa's spirit-full servant leadership touched people's hearts from all walks of life. She received numerous awards and honors, including the Nobel Peace Prize in 1979. Despite the recognition, she remained steadfast in her commitment to serving the poor and the suffering until her passing in 1997.

Mother Teresa's legacy continues to inspire millions, reminding us of the profound impact that servant leadership can have on transforming lives and fostering compassion and love for others. Her story exemplifies how a spirit-full servant leader can make a profound difference in the world through selfless service and love.

Diversity and Inclusivity

Maya Angelou was more than a revolutionary figure who shattered racial, gender, religious, and intelligence stereotypes. In addition, she was also perhaps one of the most motivating minds of the 20th century. Maya Angelou was an inspiring and spirit-filled leader who profoundly impacted literature, civil rights, and culture. While she may not have led traditional teams in a corporate sense, her leadership qualities and inspirational nature transcended boundaries. They had a positive influence on individuals and society as a whole.

Here are some ways in which Maya Angelou exemplified leadership and inspired team culture:

- **Resilience and Overcoming Adversity:** Maya Angelou's life was marked by significant challenges, including a traumatic childhood, racial discrimination, and personal struggles. Her ability to overcome these adversities showcased her resilience and determination. Her journey from a victim of trauma to a survivor and achiever is an example of turning challenges into opportunities for growth. This spirit of resilience inspired others to persevere through difficulties, fostering a sense of collective strength within the broader community.

- **Empowerment and Self-Expression:** Through her powerful poetry and writings, Maya Angelou encouraged people to embrace their identities, express themselves, and take pride in their cultural heritage. This message of empowerment resonated with many, fostering a sense of belonging and self-confidence. In a team culture, leaders who empower their members to express their unique viewpoints and talents create an environment where diversity of thought is celebrated, and innovation can thrive.

- **Inclusivity and Social Justice:** Maya Angelou advocated for civil rights and social justice, using her platform to raise awareness about inequality and discrimination. Her work highlighted the importance of inclusivity and equality, inspiring people to stand up against injustice. Leaders who champion diversity and inclusivity in their teams contribute to a culture where everyone feels valued, respected, and heard.

- **Lifelong Learning and Growth:** Maya Angelou was a lifelong learner who embraced education and personal growth. Despite her early challenges, she continued to seek knowledge and wisdom throughout her life. This commitment to learning encourages team growth, motivating members to continuously improve and develop their skills.

- **Positive Attitude and Optimism:** Maya Angelou's writings often conveyed a sense of hope and optimism, even in the face of adversity. Her ability to find light in the darkest situations was a beacon of hope for others. Leaders who maintain a positive attitude and inspire hope can uplift team morale and motivate members to tackle challenges with a constructive mindset.

Maya Angelou's leadership style was characterized by her authenticity, resilience, inclusivity, and commitment to social justice. While she may not have led teams in a traditional organizational sense, her influence extended to inspiring individuals and communities to unite, support one another, and work toward a better world. Maya was a mentor to Oprah Winfrey for many years before she passed away on May 28, 2014. Her teachings continue to resonate and encourage people to this day.

Positive Change

One spirit-full leader with a depth of vision is Malala Yousafzai. Despite facing threats and violence, her courageous advocacy for girls' education and women's rights showcases her unwavering commitment to equality.

Malala is a Pakistani education activist who gained international recognition for her unwavering commitment to promoting education, gender equality, and human rights, particularly in the face of adversity. Born in 1997 in the Swat Valley region of Pakistan, Malala's early life was marked by her passion for learning and her advocacy for girls' education in a society where women's access to education was severely limited. In 2012, at just 15 years old, she survived an assassination attempt by the Taliban while riding a bus home from school. This horrifying incident garnered global attention and turned Malala into a symbol of resilience and determination in the face of extremism and oppression.

Malala is considered a spirit-full leader because her remarkable actions embody the spirit of compassion, courage, and a deep commitment to creating positive change. Despite facing grave danger, she refused to be silenced and advocated for girls' rights to receive an education. Her advocacy led to the establishment of the Malala Fund, a nonprofit organization dedicated to ensuring 12 years of free, quality education for girls worldwide. Malala's leadership exemplifies the core principles of a spirit-full leader: her empathy for those who suffer, her unwavering commitment to justice, her resilience in the face of adversity, and her ability to inspire people globally with her message of hope and empowerment.

Malala's journey takes her from a young girl advocating for education in a remote corner of Pakistan to a globally recognized advocate for peace and equality. This journey showcases her profound spirit and depth of vision. Her leadership is a beacon of hope, encouraging individuals to stand up for their beliefs and work toward a more just and equitable world.

Commitment to Peace

Dag Hammarskjöld, the second Secretary-General of the United Nations, was not only known for his diplomatic skills and commitment to peace but also for his unique approach to leadership that was deeply rooted in spirituality. Hammarskjöld's spiritual leadership was characterized by his profound inner reflection, ethical principles, and unwavering commitment to serving humanity.

"I realize now that in comparison to him, I am a small man.
He was the greatest statesman of our century."
President John F. Kennedy on Dag Hammarskjöld after his death.

Hammarskjöld believed that true leadership required a connection to something greater than oneself. He viewed spirituality as a vital aspect of his personal and professional life, guiding his decision-making and actions. He found solace and guidance in prayer, meditation, and introspection, which helped him navigate the complex and challenging world of international diplomacy.

Central to Hammarskjöld's spiritual leadership was his unwavering commitment to ethics and integrity. He understood that leadership carried a moral responsibility, and he consistently upheld his principles, even when faced with adversity. His actions were driven by a deep sense of justice, fairness, and compassion for everyone regardless of nationality or background.

Furthermore, Hammarskjöld's leadership was characterized by his dedication to serving humanity. He believed that leaders should prioritize the well-being and dignity of every individual, striving to create a more just and equitable world. His tireless efforts to resolve conflicts, promote peace, and alleviate suffering reflected his genuine concern for the betterment of humanity.

Dag Hammarskjöld serves as a timeless example of how spirituality can shape and enhance one's leadership capabilities. His commitment to inner reflection, ethical principles, and service to humanity inspires leaders to strive for a deeper connection to their values as they navigate the world's complexities and work towards a more peaceful and just society.

Effortless action

Lao Tze, also known as Laozi, was an ancient Chinese philosopher and the reputed founder of Taoism. His teachings and spiritual views have had a profound impact on Chinese culture and philosophy.

Lao Tze's central belief revolved around the concept of the Tao, which can be loosely translated as the Way. For him, the Tao represented the natural order of the universe, the underlying principle that governs all things.

In Lao Tze's view, true wisdom and spiritual enlightenment could be attained by aligning oneself with the Tao and embracing the simplicity and spontaneity of nature. He emphasized the importance of living in harmony with the Tao and advocated for the practice of Wu Wei, which means non-action or effortless action. This concept involves allowing things to unfold naturally, without unnecessary interference or resistance.

Regarding leadership, Lao Tze proposed a distinctive approach. He believed that the best leaders were those who followed the principles of Taoism and governed with humility and compassion. Lao Tze encouraged leaders to adopt a hands-off approach, allowing people to live in accordance with their own nature and the natural rhythms of the world. He saw excessive control and intervention as detrimental, promoting instead a leadership style that was gentle, flexible, and non-coercive.

In Lao Tze's view, true leadership involves leading by example, inspiring others through one's own virtuous conduct, and fostering an environment of harmony and balance. By embodying the qualities of the Tao, leaders could cultivate trust, promote self-governance, and encourage the flourishing of their followers. Lao Tze's teachings on leadership emphasize the power of humility and mindfulness and the understanding that true strength lies in embracing the natural flow of life.

Such leaders are characterized by their unwavering commitment to ethical behavior, empathy, compassion, and a deep sense of purpose. These leaders prioritize the well-being of their teams and communities, fostering a sense of unity and shared purpose.

Let us embrace the responsibility to foster leadership that goes beyond the conventional, that uplifts and empowers those around us. Through these intentional acts of leading with a full spirit and heart, we have the collective capacity to create ripple effects leading to positive change, enriching the lives of those we touch and influencing the broader landscape of leadership in both our local communities and beyond.

"Spiritual leadership is knowing where God wants people to be and taking the initiative to get them there by God's means in reliance on God's power."

~ John Piper

Essence of the Spirit-Full Leader

Character

T he greatest gift we ever get is life itself; everything else is how we live life and use the platform we have been given. So, we choose our starting point and how to evolve from that.

The second greatest gift is the understanding that the aforementioned conclusion counts for everyone and everything else, from the smallest ant and blade of grass to your fellow human beings, and even enemies.

The third greatest gift is understanding that we share our existence on this planet with everyone else, and have the privilege to live here, not the right.

The fourth greatest gift is understanding that you come into and leave this life naked. The only thing we bring to our next life is our spirit.

The fifth greatest gift is knowing your gift is a loan, and you are here to make something of it. But not to harm anyone else.

This realization is not acquired through experience, a certain position, or reviewing facts and figures. It only emerges with a personal awakening of the spirit.

Maybe that is why many truly awakened people do not traditionally become traditional business leaders. They see more of the truth of reality and choose to take on another path instead. They do not get blinded by the headlights while driving the fast lane of life. Instead, many of them are thought leaders and act as bridges, uniting the holy in a human being with the current reality, being a spirit-full leader.

A leader's character is shaped by their spirit, and the manner in which this character manifests is influenced by their inherent nature.

The character is something we foster ourselves into; yes, we are imprinted by the circumstances in which we grow up, but we have our free will and our desires to develop our ability to become new versions of ourselves and to forge ourselves into the person we want to be. Society provides the platforms, not for everyone but for many, the schools, and libraries that anyone can use to educate themselves. It's harder for those who have started with fewer resources, but it is always possible to climb our ladder. As we said, not everyone becomes a president, but we can be a spirit-full leader in any situation or role. If we do not believe in this, we are doomed not to be able to develop beyond the beliefs of our parents and the local society we grow up in. And we consider ourselves as living proof of that.

Great leaders inherently do good. While they might not always recognize the profound gifts they possess, these gifts undoubtedly guide their actions. And it is this inner guiding, free from dogma and illusions but built on a universal common sense, driving the leaders we look up to as role models. It's their navigation.

Navigation

The spirit-full leader has a well-educated, trained, and connected GPS inside their mind.

The spirit-full leader, just out of the definition, navigates through their spirit, not through goals or circumstances. They are guided by values, great principles, universal truth, and the freedom of choice.

The Great Principles of Spirit-Full Leadership

- **Non-Violence and Non-Aggression:** Never do anything to harm anyone or anything.
- **Truth:** Be authentic with your words, and use them wisely.
- **Integrity:** Walk your talk. Never steal or cheat, not even the slightest.
- **Moderation:** Use your life force and the resources you get wisely, and be sustainable.
- **Generosity:** Be generous because nothing in this world belongs to you; it's on loan.
- **Compassion:** Remember that the other is another you.
- **Courage**: Be bold and face your fears, but not at the cost of someone else.

To grow and expand our proficiency in navigation, we need to practice every day. Like any other muscle, the spirit-full muscle also requires training and continuous practice. Even the Dalai Lama does that every day. It becomes a way of living, and it becomes you.

Some days, we will fail. Some days, we do not want to practice. We take a break and rest, just like with everything else. Rest is fundamental to growing a spiritual fullness, just as building a solid body and mind. This, too, can be challenging, like learning to ride a bike, ski, surf, or ride a motorcycle. Once you have found the keys, it will be natural.

Practices include meditation, journaling, yoga, painting, exercising, reading, singing, dancing, and gardening. Anything that integrates and connects you to yourself and your highest self, and which supports you in your expansion. One must understand that the practices do not awaken you; you awaken yourself. However, the exercises can help you stay connected and not be disconnected. When every part of your day becomes a part of your practice, that's living in ceremony, the ceremony of generating and manifesting yourself.

You will most certainly need your practice. When you start to change, your surroundings, family, and colleagues might find you odd, perhaps you will find yourself odd as well. Maybe you don't even recognize yourself anymore. But you are not weird; you are just transforming, out of the shell, into a beautiful butterfly. The people that surround you might find it scary that you've changed, while they have not. They might try to convince you that your new path is not good for you and attempt to drag you back into your previous version. But you want to upgrade to the next and higher version of yourself. So, use your practice to stay on your course.

Follow your heart, is something people say because they long for it themselves, but when someone does it, well, it can be found to be scary. It's not certain others will understand and, by that, not being supportive. So, the support might need to be found somewhere else, mostly inside yourself.

Then, you will need your routines, inspirations, and fellow travelers who can route for you when you get stuck.

Transformer

Just as the spirit-full leader is a healer, she is also a transformational leader.

When we heal, we transform; that goes for any individual, family, or organization. Healing means to put together what's been separated, making it whole. And making that which is holy unfold. When we heal, we go from one composition to another, which is a transformation. The healing starts when we allow the new version of ourselves to enter by welcoming and bringing in the new, and since healing cleans up, it also opens up a space for more of the new to enter. When we shift reality, the transformation process allows the new to enter and bring innovations, creativity, solutions, and peace.

The spirit-full leader can unfold potential. She acts as a spark that ignites, the catalyst that brings a perspective and a vision, and the moderator that guides the process in which the potential unfolds.

She brings herself to the situation, puts herself in the middle of it, and listens; from there, it starts.

The underlying structures create the situation and by changing them, unfolds the potential. The underlying means both structures we are aware of and those we are unaware of, inside and outside. The programming and patterns that create the situation in these structures are, in this sense, the composition of matter and non-matter.

The spirit-full leader can change or create underlying structures that unfold potential and influence the creation of circumstances where all life can thrive.

Awareness

Awareness is what many talk about, but few explore.

One of my previous managers and colleagues used to say, *"We should direct chance"*. I asked him, *"What do you mean?"* He said, *"Change is the unpredictable and undirected outcome of a situation. If we manage the situation well, we neutralize chance, the happening, from deciding the outcome."* I asked him, "How do you do that?" He answered, *"I listen."* I do not think he knew that what he had done was direct the energy. He did that by listening, asking questions, giving perspectives, and summarizing the discussion. He continuously asked questions like *"Is this what we have concluded to do...?"* and *"Is this what we agree...?"* and he expressed advice like, *"I suggest that we..."* Presenting open questions and advice that empowered the group.

Another story from this time took place when the whole board was in a lively discussion and could not agree. Finally, the chairman paused the conversation, stood up, and went to my colleague's office. He asked him to come to the board meeting and said they needed help with their issue. My colleague asked me to come along, and we went to the board room. When we entered, there was silence, and everybody looked at my colleague. He waited for a minute to grasp the situation before he started speaking. When he started talking, he said. *"I hear you say that..."* he then summarized their discussion neutrally, gave a perspective, and advised us on how to reach a decision. One of the board members raised his voice and said, *"That's exactly what we should do."* The others agreed, and the decision was made in a few minutes.

When we returned to our offices, my colleague turned to me and said, *"Now you know what I meant when I mentioned directing the chance. I knew about the issue they had been discussing, but I did not know the situation in the room. When I listened to the situation and let the whole situation sink in and neutralize, I knew I could give some advice."* He continued, *"Ten years back, I would probably have gone head-on into the discussion, trying to claim my viewpoint and argued. Today, I know that arguing only feeds fighting for winning, and we will all be lost in the struggle over who is right or wrong. Instead of that, we understand the situation from a broader perspective."*

I was fifteen years younger than my colleague, and just like a wise man, he did not aim it as feedback to me. Instead, he just shared his experience and looked at me with sincere concern, letting me contemplate and learn from the situation I had just experienced.

He had learned how to go heart first into the situation, and just by being there with his wisdom, he could untangle the problem.

We need to let go of self-awareness and be the sage who downloads what needs to be unfolded at the moment neutrally. Running around and proclaiming our opinions always hinders what wants to be uncovered from being seen and heard.

The bosses who are full of themselves and have all the answers, or try to manage all themselves, will soon have wiped away all initiative and creativity from their employees. I still find it mysterious that the world is full of cultures that put the boss on the pedestal because he is the boss and not because he empowers his workers, or that we elect those kinds of people to become our leaders. But most dictators fall sooner or later.

Hold Space

A great leader holds space, leads with their vision, and inspires others to achieve greatness.

We hold space by letting our spirit bring compassion and passion to the dream's "why," and intention. We hold space by allowing our energy to stabilize the ebb and flow of everyday life. Stability is not the same as being conservative; it's about being predictable, transparent, and easy to understand and follow.

When we are at our peak by holding space, we do not have a clue about the outcome, but we bless and have trust in the process that everything should turn out well, and we keep bringing our love to the intention, like bringing up a child.

When I graduated from university, my mother expressed how proud of me she was for graduating, and of how much effort I had put into my studies. I don't think she imagined of me going to the university when I was young, nor did she think of her son as someone who would one day become an author. She said, amongst many other appreciative words, *"No one has ever been able to teach you something you do not want to learn."* She meant that literally, and being my mother and a teacher, she had met quite a few young boys who had difficulty sitting still. She had a challenge when I was born to practice her patience since I was quite stubborn when there was something I did not want to do, and with a reading and writing disorder, she got a handful at home in addition to her students. So I can forgive her for chasing me through the house several times with a book, yelling, and for trying to make me read or learn something I did not want to know. But finally, she found the rip in the curtain where she could come through, and that was the fact that I loved the stories of the ancient heroes. And I learned to read by reading more and more of all the classic Roman novels.

Both my parents embrace tough love, not taking no for an answer. They also push and pull and are very supportive. They are not the type of person you could fool even if you tried; they are intuitive and have strong senses. Somehow, they gave up trying to foster me and gave in to hold the space; we pray for it to turn out well.

I have always had a strong will and solid integrity; if I did not like a situation, I would try to change it or leave it. If I did not feel appreciated, it was noticed. I have never been good at keeping my mouth shut; I'd rather voice my opinion. Mostly, that has led me to something good, but sometimes, getting into trouble makes others uncomfortable, especially if a person in a higher rank who does not like to be challenged. I did that in school and at home, and I do not have much respect for hierarchy, but I do respect character.

As I grew older, my debates with my mother became more and more tense, even to the point that they often escalated into a conflict. My personality at the time was such that I did not back down in a fight or an argument. I've learned that I had to stand up for myself and to stand my ground. Bullied in school and sensitive, I had to defend myself. I do not back down today either, but I have grown a win-win way of listening from my heart, instead of debating to win. Concerning my mother, I felt that she was not listening, and she thought that I was too stubborn and aggressive. None of us was listening to the other. We were simply defending our opinions. We were people with strong opinions and a drive to succeed.

It came to the point where I did not feel that I had my mother's love and that she did not care for me, so our relationship became very frosty. I told her what I felt about her as a mother, and of course, that hurt. Of course, it was not true that she did not love or care for me; she just had her programming triggered much like I had.

So somehow, my parents gave in to that; they had to trust that I would pave my way and that their boy had the wisdom to navigate life. So they held space, not interfering but supporting the way I went about life. They continued to give advice, speaking about values, but they had given in to the fact that they could not teach me; I could only teach myself and I had the wisdom to navigate this life.

However, the situation with my mother had forged a fighter with a drive that, if challenged, would take the fight and argue for his cause to an extent that was not always so positive. When this part of me was triggered, I could easily lose my temper, then I would draw my sword and go to battle, and I would not accept defeat. This continued for several years in my job and my relations. In these situations, I was not that humble and likable of a person. It wasn't until I had a leadership coach that said, "*You are a pain in the ass; you have to make up for your anger,*" that something changed. In that period of time, I had had several other awakenings that had started to shift me, helped me mature, and allowed me to see what relationships were all about.

Today, I can see the huge gift my relationship with my mother has been for me; it was such a huge and affecting experience. I am proud of her guts, all she has accomplished, and her creativity to take on life and hold space with my father. That relationship prepared me for leadership roles because when the dust finally settled, I had transformed. I could create with immense love, knew how to hold space, and finally, I also developed the ability to listen with an open heart.

I have made many mistakes during my life, or as I prefer to say, I have had many experiences and learned many lessons. Some went to the extent that they could have killed me, but instead, they have awakened me.

I have also been gifted with many great managers along the way, people who have seen the curious youngster with his sometimes unconventional ways of doing things, with many ideas that he has wanted to try but could not explain; he just knew. Most of the time, they have allowed me to try, though at the same time they showed some concern and offered advice while observing from a distance. They have put their reputations and results at stake without knowing what I would pull off. If I made a mess of what I tried, I would also work hard to make it right again, effectively cleaning up my own mess. The lesson is simple: Own your mistakes and learn from them. In doing so, your successes will shine even brighter, fostering trust from yourself and others. I have spent much of my career in the nuclear energy business, so it is not where you should improvise your solutions or argue to win.

Good leaders open doors and show the way; great leaders hold space and make room for experience and potential to unfold, even if uncomfortable. Spirit-full leaders shine their light on the situation, the company, the country, and the cause.

The Marketplace

If we want to test whether we are enlightened, we should go to the marketplace and stand right in the middle of it. The challenge is right there. Can we stand there without being influenced by all the ongoing energies and do our thing? Probably not, not even Jesus or Buddha could do that. We might think we are doing it, but we aren't.

Maybe we have goods that we can sell, like books. But most often, the only thing we have is ourselves. Imagine being completely naked in the marketplace, without anything more than yourself. Who are you? Maybe this scares the crap out of you. I know I was terrified.

One of the more significant challenges in today's society is not that we are theoretically uneducated; it's that we conform. We do as everyone else does. We conform to what is passable; we are mainstream. Unfortunately, we do not conform with the tiny part of the population that thinks of who they are, what they do, and, most importantly, why they do it.

Growing up on a farm, I've understood early on that our outcomes mirror our efforts—just as the seeds we sow determine the crops we harvest. If we plant potatoes, we get potatoes, and if we plant wheat, we get wheat. A potato does not become wheat. It matters how much we even try to think positively, do energy work, and pray. These things grow at the speed their DNA is designed to. I've also learned that we must do the work to get what we want. It's just a matter of how we do it and if we learn the few universal truths that control matter. We can look at our work as a burden, or we can enjoy what we have chosen. To be a farmer is to select work that never ends; it's never something you are finished with. The peak of operational excellence is the farmer who gets up in the morning and makes sure to do his utmost concerning a prosperous harvest.

Our mind is like soil; what we plant is what we get. Though what we plant is a consequence of our underlying structures, to understand what we plant, we need to contact the one inside who picks and plants the seeds, nurtures the soil, fertilizes it, and picks the weeds. Positive thinking is not enough for this; we need to get a more expansive education and learn what it is to be an energy being who lives the frequencies of the universe.

A short distance from where I live is a rock in the forest with an inscription, "When the gold speaks, all reasoning is fruitless; character is a fully educated will." Made by the landlord Alfred Bexell 1831-1900.

I had often thought of that inscription when I passed that rock during my hikes. What I think of this is that in the "marketplace" when the "gold" speaks, we tend to forget what our real gold is, and we get blinded by the "gold" we strive for, by envy, by getting more of it, we conform to what's passable. We learn many things from our parents and others in school, but I rarely hear anyone say that university has given them a fully educated will. A fully educated will, in the way I interpret Mr. Bexell, is to be the human that has come in conscious contact with her spirit and has learned how to listen to it, take guidance from it, and by this, be in relation with herself in a way that we can stand freely in the middle of the marketplace without being distorted by it or conform to it.

A spirit-full leader needs to be in full contact with her inner navigator on a level where she can navigate from cloud-free height while at the same time being firmly grounded. She will start to conform if she is caught up in the clouds. Politicians have done this during the Covid pandemic. Seeing that the other countries closed down, they felt that they had to do so too, not because it was the right thing to do, but because the others have done it and because they must've worried about what they would look like if they didn't. "We might be criticized, not elected, or worse, blamed for having another way of seeing things." Humans are copycats, whether we want to see it or not. Workers do as workers do; the rich do as the rich do, and the yoga gurus do as the yoga gurus do. We all conform one way or the other. So, when we think we are unique, we are not; we are very much alike. However, a small percentage of the population has deep concern about educating their will and will go their way, try new paths, and explore things. And they are successful because they follow their own choice deliberately.

It's not happening until we challenge ourselves to go outside our comfort zone.

The most luxurious thing I can imagine is to have the space to dwell in while going on our personal development, and that space being free. Our most luxurious assets came to us for free when we were born. And we take them for granted unless something devastating happens, like a motorcycle accident where you have a near-death experience. Maybe you awake and start to be concerned about your way of living and who you are; at least it worked that way for me.

Though it might seem trivial, my motorcycle accidents were pivotal to my awakening. Usually, people say we should shake that off, heal up, and move on. But experiencing a near-death experience is nothing you can simply shake off. To better illuminate the profound impact of these events, allow me to delve into the details.

My first near-death accident occurred when I was 20. I was on my way to see a friend and was in a bit of a hurry, a dangerous mindset for someone on a motorcycle who feels invincible. My Kawasaki 500 was a rocket, and I treated the road like a racetrack.

On the road, there was a railway crossing situated right at a turn. Leading up to this was a long straightaway with a slight bump. I usually used that bump as my braking point. However, on that particular day, I was traveling much faster than usual. The last thing I recall is trying to use the brake right before reaching the bump and then again as I rode over it. This caused the front of my bike to bottom out, rendering me unable to steer, and I quickly lost control.

Witnesses told me that as the road curved, I continued straight, crashing into the steel barrier lining the outside of the turn. The impact launched me, like Superman, into an adjacent field. Although I don't have a clear memory of the events that transpired that day, I've been informed there were about a hundred meters of skid marks on the asphalt leading up to the barrier. The one image that is still seared into my mind is that of a telephone pole rushing towards me. Then, everything faded to black, only to be replaced by an enduring, blinding white.

Bystanders witnessed the accident and called an ambulance. By the time paramedics arrived, I was "unconscious" but wandering around the field, clutching my injured arm and seemingly searching for something. They rushed me to the hospital, where I underwent surgery and eventually regained consciousness in the intensive care unit about 12 hours later. My injuries included a broken right arm, severed ligaments in my thumb, a concussion, and numerous stitches in my forehead from where my helmet had shattered upon impact. Beyond that, my body bore the signs of severe trauma, but miraculously, no other significant injuries. Awakening from that enveloping white light was utterly surreal. It felt as though I'd journeyed somewhere else and had now returned to my physical form. At the same time, of course, I had a lot of painkillers in my system.

The second accident occurred when I was 24. After some years, I purchased another motorcycle. This time around, I was driving much more cautiously, yet I couldn't resist the allure of the ride; it invigorated me, giving a sense of life. The thrill of speed, the adrenaline, the sense of control over the vehicle. This particular accident didn't occur at a high speed. I was riding with some friends on a small backcountry road. Misjudging a turn, I veered a bit wide and the gravel on the road caused me to lose the front-end grip. I managed to straighten the bike, but this caused me to overshoot the turn. Attempting to stop, I steered into a ditch. Hidden there was a concrete drainpipe, obscured by grass. I collided with it, catapulting over the handlebars, heading straight for a large rock. In that fleeting moment, I thought, "This is the end." Darkness ensued, soon replaced by a blinding white light.

Instinctively, I stretched my arms out in defense. My hands and head made first contact with the rock. From a detached perspective, it felt as if I watched myself perform a somersault over the rock, eventually landing back on the road and then into the ditch a few meters beyond. Throughout, I remained eerily aware, completely present in the moment. The landing fractured my thighbone and the sharp rock cut my hands. I found myself face-first in the ditch, slowly regaining full consciousness. My friends who were ahead of me did not notice my accident. They continued for some kilometers before they noticed. But by some fortunate twist of fate, a passing couple found me. The woman, an emergency nurse, administered immediate care and called for an ambulance. Given the dangers of a fractured thighbone, her timely intervention was a blessing. When my friends came back, they supported by keeping calm, present, and held my hand to calm my pain as the medical staff lifted me onboard. The little tour had ended in chock.

There are plenty more tales intertwined with these traumatic events, each having its unique impact on me. For instance, during the first accident, my father happened to be driving home on the same road. He witnessed the pickup truck extracting my mangled motorcycle from the field, and the shock he felt upon recognizing the bike is indescribable. From the surgeon's skill in repairing my thigh to the unwavering support from the hospital staff and friends, the compassion and concern were palpable. And then there was a girl, someone I'd recently met. She waited in the emergency room until I awoke post-surgery. The very same girl expressed her anger after my second accident but chose to remain by my side. Today, she is my beloved wife.

It's a trauma to nearly lose the most precious gift you have got, your life. Surviving once with just a broken arm is fortunate; doing so twice feels miraculous. Both times, I saw the end coming towards me, and in a flash, I came back, but after my body had been badly bruised, my consciousness opened on a new level.

This made me aware that guardians are watching over us; for me, there is no doubt. As a young man, I lived partly like I had a death wish, throwing myself into things I was not ready for and mostly at speeds far beyond my capacity. I did not understand that it was a wish to live and to feel life; there was so much life running in my veins that it was pumping.

After the second crash, I got into some life panic; I had to do everything right. I could not waste any moment and lived to the fullest, but in a new way. I enjoyed everyday situations in a way others could not understand. Living to the fullest, in my sense, was not about partying. It was a thirst to fully experience life: to savor its tastes, breathe in its aromas, soak in every experience, and realize my utmost potential. But it was the kick in the butt that got me going. I went to university, made a career, and became a leader. It was like I had been shot out of a cannon. Experience after experience came over me at a speed that I could hardly manage. I both pushed hard and struggled with myself during these years. This continued for many years until the experience of real peace entered.

Looking back at these accidents from another perspective made me see them as gifts. They could be seen as useless accidents that only bring pain and hurt, but if we give them time and attention, they might reveal something much greater about ourselves. One of the gifts these accidents have given me is that my body hurts as soon as

I am on the wrong track in life. It's an incredible signal system the human body has, if you only listen.

Not many have the time and space to allow themselves to dwell in their personal development because most of us are busy making a living, surviving, or maybe too occupied making a career and don't give time to reflect on what is happening, to listen to both the subjective and the objective world. You who read this book probably belong to the tiny percentage of the world's population that can afford personal development such as coaching, therapy, or a course. You probably belong to the even smaller percentage that does so because otherwise, you probably would not have read this book.

A friend used to say, "Nothing is too expensive when you invest in yourself." Well, my interpretation of that is to spend time on my personal development. Self-realization has become a word afflicted by ego and selfishness, but the true meaning is a thoroughly educated will, an awakened soul in full realization. It is free of charge, and we must give it our attention.

The spirit-full leader knows to train and fully educate her will, connect with the higher self, and act heart first. That's a fully educated will, and then the "gold" can speak in any language it wants, but you will feel rich regardless. Follow your chosen path, and you will probably be very comfortable in leadership.

"Leadership is not about you; it's about investing in the growth of others."

~ Ken Blanchard

Spirit-Full Leadership with God

S pirit-full leadership is like general leadership in that it has many of the same ideas but has some unique parts that must be understood and used. Spirit-full leaders guide others to connect with their highest selves. The Holy Spirit guides spirit-full leaders. God asks spirit-full leaders to do what only He can do. Only the Holy Spirit can alter people's spirits; spirit-full leaders. Instead, the Spirit uses individuals to help others develop spiritually.

Spirit-full leadership is discerning God's will for a group of people and then taking charge in applying God-honoring strategies to that group while trusting in God's ability to bring about the desired results. In a spiritual state and a way of life that shows off His splendor and brings credit to His name, that's where God wants people to be.

It might surprise you that I'm not deeply religious, and I have always felt that God helps those who help themselves. One effective approach to self-help is nurturing our highest potential, which aligns with living according to God's wisdom. The recent passing of my father strengthened my bond with God, deepening my spiritual practice of breathwork, meditation, yoga, and nurturing my chakras.

In the later stages of his life, my dad underwent a profound transformation, embracing a journey of faith supported by his wife. I had the privilege of sharing precious moments with him before he departed from this earthly realm. Despite Parkinson's disease having gradually taken away his ability to articulate more than a mumble or a few coherent words, an unexpected gift emerged—the heightened capacity to experience and express profound emotions, particularly love. In those final weeks of his life, I encountered a depth of paternal love that surpassed any previous experience. It was as if the essence of his love, akin to a gentle mist of rain, enveloped me, opening my heart to a level of connection and spirituality that resonates profoundly within the framework of spirit-full leadership.

At the core of spirit-full leadership lies a profound aspiration—to guide and support individuals in fostering a personal relationship with God, channeling their lives toward a purpose that glorifies the divine. The essence of spirit-full leadership is not merely centered around traditional notions of directing or commanding; rather, it is rooted in the transformative power of influence. Spirit-full leaders, therefore, aim not to dictate but to inspire and shape the spiritual journeys of those under their guidance.

This chapter explores the facets of spirit-full leadership, unraveling the qualities that elevate a leader from having a mere influence, to greatness. This shift in focus recognizes that the essence of leadership is not solely measured by the size of the crowd one leads but by the depth of the spiritual connection fostered and the transformative influence wielded by the leader in the lives of those they touch.

A great spirit-full leader, then, is one whose teachings echo with timeless wisdom, leaving an indelible mark on the hearts and minds of their followers. The measure of respect for such a leader transcends mere popularity, delving into the profound impact of their spiritual insights. This exploration aims to uncover the characteristics, principles, and practices that contribute to making a spirit-full leader whose influence is marked not by authority alone but by the enduring wisdom that guides and uplifts those who choose to walk the spiritual path alongside them.

Unconditional Love

The potent elixir of love, trust, care, and compassion may alter a person's perceptions and values in ways that nothing else can. So why wouldn't this also be true for spiritual leadership?

Isn't leadership about getting others to believe in and act on goals that seem out of reach?

If a leader wants to spark this movement, they must address their followers' most fundamental desires. The wish to be loved without conditions, trusted, respected, and cared for without reservations.

However, we know that mammalian design causes the brain to shut down all of its capabilities whenever danger is in sight. Hence, it's hard to see how a leader could ever gain the loyalty of their followers by resorting to force.

What factors will affect unconditional love?

Possibly unyielding confidence in the honesty of those in authority. The most powerful ways to change behavior, build relationships, solve problems, and get people to do their best are through intense listening, genuine empathy, and divine compassion. This is because they create an environment where people feel loved, trusted, empowered, and motivated to find solutions to problems. Building a solid community and trust between leaders and their followers is key.

On the other hand, it encourages the leaders to speak their minds openly without fear of punishment or judgment (I compared this to shooting bullets into the sand, which disappear without a trace once they've hit the ground). When people don't have to worry about how their actions may affect others' views of them, they are free to express their true thoughts and feelings without holding back.

This frees people to reach their full potential.

The best definition of leadership I've ever heard is the act of building a beautiful, symbolic cathedral or temple to encourage people to thrive in its infinite and unarguable invocation of trust, faith, and justice. Outstanding examples of this are Jane Goodall and Greta Thunberg, who are likened to cathedral builders in their commitment to sustainable and harmonious coexistence with nature. Their efforts inspire trust in the possibility of a healthier planet, faith in sustainable practices, and a commitment to justice in safeguarding the environment for future generations.

Love as an Action

It has been argued that love is the ultimate value and leadership is not. To that end, I wholeheartedly concur. Neglecting love in favor of focusing on leadership is a risk. However, if we place too much value on affection, we risk undervaluing the role of leadership. A lousy leader is a spouse who directs his wife but shows little affection for her. Even more so, a spouse who only tells his wife he loves her but never takes charge shows her that he cares little for her.

Putting love first is the essence of spirit-full leadership. Excellent leadership is an expression of love for others. Love in action is the highest kind of leadership and is the ultimate goal of every good leader. In an intriguing teaching, Jesus equated leadership with serving others and said true love means dying for others. As it turns out, love and leadership are the same; they cannot be separated.

The individuals I am tasked with guiding and serving are more important to me than my ego. Even if they started out wanting to be leaders because they wanted to be good at it, the thing that makes the best leaders stand out is their love for the people they serve.

We need to lead with love, for love, and through love. Only through our actions and decisions may we come to know and experience love. Likewise, leadership does not solve this problem. The essence of love is not solitary; it manifests through interactions and shared experiences.

According to many spiritual texts, God is love. The bond between the Father, the Son, and the Holy Spirit is the wellspring, the source, and the channel of infinite love. Therefore, to be made in God's image is to be made in love. To put it simply, God loves us. Yet, it must also be lovingly crafted. Therefore, we have the ability and the drive to love one another since it is a part of our design.

Spirit-full leaders, therefore, are welcomed by people who are loved by God and made with the desire to receive and give love. Our guiding principle is love in action. The highest calling of leadership is to create a culture based on love. When love is present, things like forgiveness, joy, peace, wisdom, creativity, humility, patience, compassion, truth, bravery, kindness, gratitude, and generosity grow.

Declaring that love is the highest calling of leadership means acknowledging that it comes at a tremendous cost. Giving up one's life for anybody, friend or foe alike is not simple. Putting the needs of others before your own is hard. Misunderstandings and criticism are inevitable. That's why it won't be recognized or valued at the time. However, love can accept this fact before it has any personal experience with it. The leader makes the vow to lead with love in mind, with love as the goal and love as the means. Putting love first is the essence of leadership. Spirit-full leadership is, and always will be, love in action for those who are called and choose to lead correctly.

Innovative Leadership

To be a spirit-full leader with a creative vision, you must learn to listen to God and people to figure out what God is up to. Then, while conceptualizing and organizing, you surrender to and align with him.

You're certain that God will lead you on a brand-new path, and you're willing to trust that He'll utilize your words, thoughts, and plans to get you there. Therefore, you should be able to declare, "It looked good to the Holy Spirit and us" (as in Acts 15:28) when you take this next step. We can find out what God wants by praying together and discussing it. Then, we can move forward bravely and creatively.

What kind of leader encourages new ideas and approaches?

An inventive leader can succeed in any setting. Leaders who think outside the box understand their position in the home (and the business) and pray together to learn God's plan so that they may act wisely. This is exemplified best by Truett Cathy, the founder of Chick-fil-A, known for his innovative business strategies and commitment to incorporating Christian values into his company's culture. Cathy believed in the importance of understanding one's role as a business leader and a person of faith. Chick-fil-A's success and unique approach to customer service reflects his outside-the-box thinking and reliance on prayer for guidance.

Gratitude

Hearing thank you is one of life's few true pleasures. A simple show of gratitude is something entirely different. To express gratitude, we must acknowledge that another person has helped us in a way we could not. To me, thankfulness is the essential spiritual discipline a human can develop and exhibit. To have experienced grace is to be grateful, and to understand grace is to have gratitude happen often in one's life.

The spirit of gratitude is central to every spirit-full leader.

Being grateful is recognizing the benefits of our good fortune and accepting them with enthusiasm.

The Value of Thank You Notes vs. Simply Hearing Their Appreciation.

"Thank you" is more than just a catchphrase we drill into our kids' heads; it's an attitude that requires constant attention and practice. Gratitude is the recognition of our need for God and other people. Self-made men are seen as arrogant and egotistical. On our own, we are unable to do much. Every major accomplishment in my life has resulted from collaborative work. Gratitude's archenemy, selfish ambition, and entitlement are constant companions in a world where we often struggle for all we have.

Energy Enhancing Activities

Developing inner spiritual strength is synonymous with developing outer physical strength via exercise. As you work on your spiritual strength, your inner spirit and connection to God are activated. This gives you the courage to live a meaningful and happy life. Even if you already have a full and happy life, spiritual practices will only improve it.

Spiritual exercise is similar to working out your muscles; it opens up your energy channels, allowing positive emotions like love and joy to flood your whole being. In time, you'll be able to put unfavorable emotions and events in the past. Incorporating positive energy exercises into your daily routine will profoundly impact your mood.

Boost your faith with these seven physical and mental exercises:

1. Surround yourself with supportive people who care about you.

Is there anything about your relationships that you want to change?

It is your fate to be happy and content in this life, especially with people you care about. When people are spiritually grounded, God will always protect them from harm. While it's true that certain discouraging ideas may pop into your head, you may allow your spiritual fortitude to do the talking for you, much like a bodyguard.

You should do something to demonstrate your appreciation for the people you care about. For example, a phone call or an email may go a long way toward making someone feel special. It can be a turning point in their day.

2. Take as many breaks outdoors as possible.

Increasing your spiritual fortitude is as simple as spending more time in nature. Growing ties to the Earth and the natural world help one become more in tune with the source of all life. It's a fast track to the divine, opening the floodgates for good vibes to flow through you.

As you spend more time outdoors, pay greater attention to nature's sounds and sights. Tune into the kinetics of the wind blowing by you and take a deep whiff of your environment. So many different aspects of nature may appeal to your senses and make you happy.

3. Minimize disruptions (TV, Radio, Internet, Newspaper).

The media may flood your head with many commercials, shows, and events, but the vast majority are irrelevant to achieving your full potential. When you cut down on your time on these activities, your brain is exposed to less artificial stimulation and gets a chance to rest in peace. You may use this time of reflection to deepen your spiritual connection with yourself and others.

And if you're not ready to give them up or cut down on them (we get it), then at least attempt to focus your attention on the things you want to see rather than the ones you don't.

4. Watch what you think about the people in your life.

It's crucial to provide and accept good vibes from others around you. There's no use in passing judgment on other people since you will be held accountable for your conduct. Negative feelings and thoughts, like pain, gossip, fear, and hopelessness, don't do anyone any good and serve no purpose.

A person's vibe may either propel them forward in the face of difficulty or cause them to falter and collapse. Take the high road and treat everyone with compassion. Recognize the goodness (and God) inside them and do everything you can to enhance that goodness so it can guide them to their greatest existence. You have no clue what type of war they are waging right now, but the positive vibes you send their way are invaluable.

5. Have trust and take a chance.

Have the confidence to keep going even when things become tough. Trust that God has your back and that a greater breakthrough lies beyond the difficulties you are now facing. When you stand up or speak out, knowing that your faith is stronger than your fear, the idea that fear is trying to hold you back will fade and go away. When you take a leap of faith, you gain strength and maturity. Everyone and everything we encounter serves as a teacher and a test; use the opportunity to your advantage.

6. Consider the needs of others before your own.

A review of historical examples reveals that the most spiritually powerful, serene, and loving people were those who dedicated their lives to helping others. True strength and tranquility may be found in selfless service. Make an effort to aid fellow human beings or at least contact someone who can. You don't have to be extraordinary to change someone else's life; everyone you meet is in your path for a purpose.

If you put yourself in a position of service, you will feel more spiritually empowered.

7. Make praying and meditating routines.

Your life will change if you regularly pay attention to your invisible guides, angels, or deities that are always with you. In addition, praying or meditating (whichever practice you like) at least twice a day is an excellent way to strengthen your spirit.

Most forms of prayer and meditation begin with a formal address to a higher power, such as "Dear God," "Dear Heavenly Father," or "Oh Great Healing Spirit."

Be silent while you pray or meditate, and let God fill you with power and light. Keep your requests upbeat by focusing on restoration instead of healing, plenty instead of lack, and so on. Taking the time to notice when negative energy is in your life is the first step to getting rid of it. Then, douse it with nothing but good vibes!

Don't forget to arrange regular times for this spiritual practice and do your best to keep to that schedule. This self-discipline proves to God that you mean business. But you may connect with the divine anytime you wish, via prayer and meditation or by reminding yourself, vocally or mentally, that you are always one. If you stick with this practice of spiritual fortitude, your self-belief and confidence naturally increase.

Make a plan for yourself based on these things, and keep your mind set on the goal of building your spiritual strength. Your life will gradually improve as you put in the effort required. And you'll discover that you have even more inner fortitude than you ever thought possible. Having spiritual fortitude tells you you're heading in the correct direction.

Discerning Eye

In its broadest sense, discernment is seeing and responding to God's presence and activity in every part of life, from the smallest details to the biggest decisions. Paul says, "We must change by having our thoughts renewed to know and do God's good, acceptable, and perfect will." (Rom 12:2). This applies to both the collective consciousness and the minds of individuals.

Discernment is the ability to tell the difference between two options or processes. Spiritual discernment is the ability to tell the difference between good and evil or between God, which pulls us closer to God and that which is not of God and draws us away from Him. Effective leadership depends on many things, but spiritual leadership is a commitment to follow God's plan with the help of the Holy Spirit.

In other words, corporate discernment or spirit-full leadership discernment is the ability of a group of leaders to sense the presence and activity of God in the problems we are facing and to make decisions based on what they see.

Even though it seems obvious that spirit-full leaders should be interested in finding and carrying out God's plan, many organizations don't have a clear mandate and goal. This begs the question, "What are we doing if we are not actively seeking the will of God as a community? Independently exerted? Based on our analysis and preparation, what makes the most sense? What is just a matter of strategy, what is just a matter of convenience, and what is just good for one's pride?"

On the other hand, learning to use collective discernment as leaders opens us up to a new world where we can access divine knowledge beyond what we can understand. This kind of leadership is difficult because it calls us to abandon our dependence on rational thought and plans in favor of attentiveness to the Holy Spirit at work inside and around us.

This does not mean that intuition and planning are useless. God has given us the capacity to reason and to use that reasoning to make decisions. Still, the Scriptures make it plain that human knowledge and God's wisdom are not the same, and developing discernment involves learning to tell them apart (1 Cor 1:18–31).

Since boards and other organizations with a lot of power are usually made up of hard-nosed businesspeople and realists, figuring out who should lead might be subjective or even mystical. Of course, relying on what feels like a more subjective approach in our personal lives is one thing. Still, it's a whole other ballgame when dealing with large budgets, other people's financial investments, the livelihoods of multiple employees, reports to influential boards, and the needs of a customer base (congregation or organization) with varying degrees of expectation.

Humility

In God's kingdom, leadership is not contingent on holding a position of authority. Serving others humbly is a sign of greatness in God's sight. Spirit-full leadership seeks to serve from a place of humility. Serving God and others is a great way to show humility as a leader. Being humble is laying down your life so that others may see God's love for them reflected in us.

To lead with humility, you must consider your team the only one selected by God. This means prioritizing your team members' needs and making yourself accessible to help them through challenging situations at work or home.

A humble act of leadership is investing in the next generation of leaders through mentoring or coaching. To have a humble heart for service, you must recognize the gifts God has given other young leaders and encourage the next generation to look for God's word and use it in their lives.

My observation has led me to conclude that all leaders have a selfless disposition. It's the conviction that God's will should be carried out on Earth just as in heaven. The practice of treating people as God's prized creation and serving them accordingly.

I've met and worked with people in high-level jobs who never bring themselves up in discussion. These leaders never talk about them but instead focus on other people. They may make you feel like you're the only one in the room at any given time.

Do you know a leader who exemplifies such modesty? How have they influenced your approach to leadership and service?

The foundation of a humble leadership style is a firm spiritual practice. A leader with a genuine heart, one that has given themselves up to daily spiritual nourishment, knows our ability to lead and our need for nothing more than a connection to God to fulfill those roles.

Team Culture

Whether it be the church, a sports team, a company, a school, a nonprofit, a government agency, a bank, the military, or any other institution, having a group of capable leaders at the helm is essential.

Establishing and maintaining a strong leadership team is crucial for long-term survival and the propagation of spirit-full leadership in a community.

There is no such thing as a lesser person, but neither does team leadership render a single director or manager superfluous. They possess every skill and talent required of good leaders as a group. Director authority will be defined, and team members' responsibilities will be detailed. As a group, this kind of group of leaders could reach any of the task's goals.

For example, the director of the team of five communicates with the leaders, who each take on some of the tasks to complete the project. In the aforementioned scenario, there are essentially four channels of interaction. When five people work together and engage with one another, they may open up ten communication channels. Often, all it takes to finish a specific job on time is a small group of people working well together.

Cultural Diversity

Now is the time to investigate diversity.

It's no secret that several hypotheses as to the origins of cultural differences have been proposed. These explanations range from people's religious beliefs and worldviews to their daily social and political conditions. Almost all these theories shed light on a certain truth, but they become one-sided when treating it as absolute. They both seek to answer the same issue (what accounts for these cultural differences? Furthermore, the theories do not provide explicit standards to assess what is right and wrong in any particular culture.

The biblical stance that God reveals Himself and information about creation to all people and nations provides a good starting point for our search for solutions to cultural diversity (Romans 1: 19,20). Our second main argument is that all people, regardless of their religious beliefs, are ultimately responsible to God. For the third part of our argument, we will focus on the three fundamental connections God has designed every person to have.

- God.
- The natural world.
- Connection with other people on the planet.

This requires harmony among the three connections. From a global perspective, Indian culture (as seen in Hinduism and Buddhism) places absolute emphasis on the divine or the supernatural. Everything you see, including yourself, others, and the natural world, is an illusion. True reality and significance lie in the divine. The term Pantheism (the belief that everything is divine) comes to mind while considering this approach.

The natural world (Taoism) and the Earth are essential in other East Asian traditions, such as Chinese culture. This point of view, which places excessive value on man's connection with nature, may be characterized as Naturalism.

In Africa, an individual's connection to their fellow human beings is valued highly. The individual is meaningless outside of a group, and the group is more important than any one member. This perspective may be characterized as communist.

Conversely, Western culture is the exact opposite. Each person is emphasized throughout. A human being is an individual, not a member of a group. The term Individualism characterizes this outlook.

All four civilizations (China, Africa, India and the West) value real connections with other people, so each must have some truth. However, they put too much weight on one of the three relationships and not enough on the others, which is wrong and shows a lack of understanding. I know that I am being very general by giving this overview of the three different cultures. For instance, Naturalism is more compatible with Taoism than Confucianism in China. Taoism is a religion and a way of life that places a premium on adherence to and reverence for nature's faultless rules. Conversely, Confucianism places a premium on social interaction and harmony, much like in Africa.

Getting rid of a false perception is crucial as well. It's not true that people in China or Africa have no concept of or appreciation for individualism, just as it's not true that Westerners have no concept of or appreciation for community.

Each of the three types of culture is experienced in many different ways by different groups around the world. Many Chinese people already agree with the Western value of individualism, especially business people (both at work and in their relationships with family and friends). Some white people in the West, especially in rural areas or the south of Europe, tend to be more communalist. On the other hand, many Africans, especially those living in cities and heavily influenced by the West, tend to act more like individuals.

Some civilizations we meet are hybrids, combining elements of different worldviews. Culture isn't a fixed entity but rather one that undergoes constant evolution.

In recognizing that culture is not a fixed entity but an ever-evolving phenomenon, we acknowledge the challenges posed by today's global community, where once-separate cultures now interact and influence each other. As spirit-full leaders navigate this interconnected world, understanding, appreciation, and a commitment to harmony among diverse perspectives become crucial for fostering a truly global team/organization that celebrates the richness of cultural diversity.

In essence, spirit-full leaders understand that the call to embody leadership is rooted in love, humility, gratitude, discernment, and a commitment to fostering positive team cultures in diverse settings.

"Effective spirit-full leadership is rooted in humility, empathy and a deep understanding of human nature."

~ Unknown

Healing Our Inner World

——◇○《○》○◇——

E veryone needs some form of emotional healing, especially if you are to become a leader with spiritual sustenance. Unfortunately, it's a gift that too few give to themselves. If you are anything like me, you'll leave things to the last minute or wait until things are terrible before addressing them. On one particular occasion in my life, I was sick and tired of self-medicating my emotional pain with drugs and alcohol. I had no idea how to deal with my childhood wounds or even how to process some significant emotional events that had been swept underneath the carpet, never to be seen again. It was like strolling through a massive warehouse in the dark with a small flashlight, trying to find a cure for my emotional pain.

Have you ever sensed that the currents of life were flowing beyond your influence? A lingering challenge persisted despite participating in various personal development programs, and I grappled with identifying its root cause. Despite running a successful business, certain facets of my life lacked harmony. The connections in my relationships failed to provide the support necessary to realize my fullest potential. Moreover, my family dynamics were strained. Have you ever found yourself yearning for change, only to be daunted by the unknown, thereby opting for the familiarity of the status quo? This encapsulated the juncture in my life, navigating the path where spirit-full leadership beckoned for transformative shifts.

Many underestimate the courage to ask for help when aspects of our lives aren't the way we want them to be. Tired of negative emotions driving my life, I found a healer named Simonne who works with many modalities to heal the emotional body. I was seeking a quick fix to my pain, and I had no idea that healing is a journey. Our wounds have many layers.

The modality that Simonne used most was Reiki, a soft and gentle way to help someone develop a relationship with their wounds instead of resisting them. I had been holding on to a lot of emotional pain in my heart. It was a challenging and painful experience to explore the emotions surrounding my wounds. Even now, some fifteen years later, I find it challenging to explain the healing experience that I received. We never spoke about where the pain came from. She explained that it was just a story and didn't matter. After every session, it felt like I was receiving open-heart surgery. I've come to understand that our wounds aren't necessarily our fault, but it is our responsibility to heal them. I ended up doing ten sessions with Simonne, and she opened me up to another level of sensitivity within myself.

Simonne introduced me to the power of meditation. I wasn't as consistent back then as I am today. She also suggested that I attend a meditation group aligned with John of God, a Brazilian crystal healer who works with benevolent entities to cure people of all kinds of illnesses.

I went along to a group session one evening. I had never seen anything like that before. The group meditation was in a community hall in the Eastern Suburbs of Sydney. In the center of the room was a giant crystal surrounded by a bunch of smaller ones inside a circle of candles. There were already people lying on the timber floorboards with pillows and blankets. The facilitators were a married couple, Dean and Nicole, in their early forties. I received a warm welcome, and they asked me if I had any crystals to place around theirs so they could be charged. I said no, not knowing what on earth they were talking about.

I thought, *I don't know what they are discussing, but I would like to find out.*

After claiming a spot on the floor, Dean explained that he would take us on a journey. I immediately felt safe. I began to experience meditation more profoundly than ever before. The sense that other entities were in the room was strong and undeniable. I felt loved and supported, as well as having a deep sense of appreciation and understanding that the entities were angelic.

I saw in my mind's eye a bright, warm star. As it came closer, I could feel its loving aura, and I began to cry. I received a message from this angel in a way that I could only describe as the feeling that it was playing with me like a cheeky monkey that had stolen my banana and was now teasing me. The communication was a telepathic experience, no different from hearing someone's thoughts, and it was just as precise. The angel giggled while saying I shouldn't take my wounds so seriously. I telepathically replied that my heart hurts, and it giggled, tickling my heart. Then, the pain instantly disappeared and was replaced with a warm, loving sensation. The tears continued to flow. With an encounter like that, I realized we are supported beyond anything we could have imagined. Life is conspiring to help us!

The door was now open, and I had more encounters with these angelic beings. One came as a warning voice while I was working, stating that I would be involved in a serious car accident if I wasn't careful. About two hours later, I narrowly avoided a serious car accident. Alerted, I beeped my horn when the driver of a white van was perving on a chick in a bikini and, in doing so, ran a red light. He missed my pickup by an inch or less. We were eyeball-to-eyeball. I thanked my angels for that!

My subsequent encounter came while I meditated later that same year on a warm summer night. At this point, I had my crystal collection in the center of my lounge room, surrounded by candles. In deep meditation, the blind on the kitchen window started flapping as if a strong wind was blowing, but no such breeze was coming through the balcony door, which was open and in front of the lounge room facing the same direction as the kitchen window. I felt the most benevolent energy enter the room. It was so strong that I had to open my eyes. To my amazement, almost all the fish from my aquarium were over to one side of the tank, and the angelic energy was making the fish go up and down. You can imagine the astonishment at the sight before my very eyes. All of a sudden, my brain kicked in, questioning the safety of the experience. I felt some fear, and the angelic beings were gone.

I sensed that while the scars from emotional, physical, and sexual abuse might never completely vanish, they no longer dictate the course of my life today. In its perpetual unfolding, life bears various dimensions that necessitate letting go and healing. I viewed these moments as opportunities to deepen my connection with myself—a chance to realign my path, delve into profound layers of my identity, and ascertain the essentials required for thriving in this existence.

To emerge as influential leaders capable of navigating challenging decisions and guiding others, it becomes imperative to embark on a journey of self-healing, particularly addressing the wounds of our inner child. By undertaking this personal healing process, we safeguard against inadvertently projecting our unresolved issues onto others, preventing the accidental emotional spillover that might impact those we lead. This commitment to healing fosters our well-being and lays the foundation for compassionate and empathetic leadership, creating a space where our decisions are rooted in clarity and emotional balance rather than the echoes of past wounds.

Developing A Healing Attitude

In Sonia Choquette's audiobook *Trust Your Vibes at Work*, she talks about six-sensory living instead of the five-sensory life. The five senses are, of course, sight, smell, touch, taste, and sound. She mentions the differences between trusting your intuition—six-sensory living—and being guided by your five senses. One of the main differences she shares is that when someone living from their six senses meets a new person, they think of the connection with the focus being you and me and how I can help you. When we live in our five senses and meet a new person, we think, is this person safe? The focus is on me versus you, and you scare me.

Six-sensory living creates a whole new paradigm of being, one of trust and connection, first with ourselves and then with others. It's a way of life that is healing. Most people need to see before they believe rather than believing and then seeing. We can't necessarily trust our five senses. They tell us the earth is flat, that a wave crashing on the beach is coming towards us when in reality it is moving away, and a movie isn't moving at all but is a series of still frames shown quickly at more than 400 frames per second which gives us an illusion of a film. It's a fallacy that our judgments keep us safe; they keep us from connecting, understanding, and experiencing the fullness of life. It's through fear and suppression of our uniqueness that we create dis-ease; it's an emotional pain that leads to people hurting others, eating the wrong foods, and not exercising.

At the back of Louise Hay's groundbreaking book *You Can Heal Your Life*, she shares various diseases that people experience and the multiple fears that are causing the diseases. For example, lower back pain is associated with the fear of lack, not having enough, and not feeling supported. The inspiration for Louise to write her book came from her healing journey.

From a young age, Louise was repeatedly sexually abused by her mother's boyfriend. Naturally, she was resentful of the painful experience and developed cervical cancer as a result. One of the fantastic things she did was take ownership of the disease. Louise said to herself, "I chose to have resentful thoughts. Therefore, I created this disease in my body. That means I can heal myself of cancer."

Mind you, that was in the late '70s when cancer was considered a death sentence. Instead of having an operation, she stalled for time and went to work on changing her thoughts, which had created the disease in the first place. She took full responsibility for her healing. When you change your thoughts, you change the way you feel. Essentially, Louise cured herself of cancer with her thoughts. Her book, *You Can Heal Your Life*, has sold over 40 million copies worldwide. She died of natural causes in 2017 when she was 90. Her publishing company, Hay House, has reached millions of people worldwide and published authors like Dr. Wayne Dyer, Doreen Virtue, Greg Braden, and thousands more. She was a spirit-full leader who put her words into action—showing that she meant what she said by actively doing it herself.

Dr. Wayne Dyer was another great spirit-full teacher who died in his sleep years before Louise. In his book *Wishes Fulfilled*, he talks about his diagnosis of chronic lymphocytic leukemia and his journey of healing from this disease. Dr. Dyer talks about living from the end as if you are already healed. Wayne shares his story of the remote healing he received from John of God, where he was told to fast for a week, only drinking water with herbs. On a specific time of a particular day, he was told to lie down, and the healing would begin. He awoke feeling great and decided to go for a morning walk along the beach despite being told to rest for a week. Halfway along the beach, Dr. Dyer collapsed, and a friend assisted him back to his beachside bungalow. After sleeping intermittently for a week, Dr. Wayne Dyer declared he was healed. Being such an influential person, his example elevates the belief of what is possible for others on their healing journeys.

A positive attitude and belief alone may not heal you, but they open the way for healing to find you in the form of a recommendation, as was the case with Dr. Dyer and the healing he received from John of God. Often, people are in denial of the dis-ease they feel, working long hours stressed out to the max. I find that when I've allowed myself to work long hours, I was suppressing pain that I wasn't ready to face. In many cases, working is a form of avoidance and denial of underlying dis-ease, particularly when immersed in demanding work schedules and heightened stress levels. Reflecting on personal experiences, I've observed that overworking is a band-aid used to suppress past emotional pain that requires acknowledgment and a readiness to confront for genuine healing to unfold.

Confronting aspects of our lives that no longer serve us require a certain level of vulnerability. It entails opening ourselves up to the discomfort of acknowledging and addressing elements that may have been veiled or ignored. In spirit-full leadership, embracing vulnerability becomes a strength, allowing for genuine self-awareness and paving the way for transformative growth and healing. Spirit-full leaders exhibit this vulnerability, creating an authentic and compassionate environment, fostering connections, and promoting a culture where team members feel empowered to address and transcend aspects of their lives that hinder their well-being and potential.

Past Life Regression

In early 2012, a friend of mine was a member of a Toastmasters club affiliated with Scientology. When he invited me, I thought, *why not?* I learned from attending many of Dr. Wayne Dyer's talks that having a mind that is open to everything and closed to nothing is healthy. I enjoyed the experience so much that I became a regular guest at their fortnightly meetings. They were a fun, nonjudgmental group that welcomed me with open arms. After several months of hearing my friend's many tales of transformation, I took their test and did their entry-level Dianetics program. The course was over a weekend, and I was delighted to learn that the main point of focus was past-life regression work.

At this point, I had already read *Many Lives, Many Masters* by Brian Weiss and had attended his talk at the Hay House event, "You Can Do It." I'd also had a past-life regression session in Las Vegas with a spiritual guru who had lived and studied in India for many years. I found the experience with him valuable, giving me a deeper understanding of why I do what I do. The guy was a likable character, and the regression work was far more profound than I had ever experienced before. I could actually see the past life and what I was doing. The guru and I mediated together, and he fell into my past lives and articulated them to me, relating to certain behavioral traits I thought only I knew about. It was a healing and liberating experience and enabled me to stop taking on other people's energy, spend more time in the sun, and not beat myself up for not having a partner and children. These were profound healings from one session, I would say.

The Dianetics weekend showed me the history behind my challenges with my knees. Up until that weekend, I'd had issues with my knees, even having surgery to remove damaged cartilage, and I would experience pain in my knees consistently. After my past life and pre-natal experiences with Scientology, I rarely, if ever, had knee complaints.

If you are as curious about life as I am, you may wonder what happened. I went back to live in the 16th or 17th century. The streets were paved with cobblestones. I held my mother's hand as she held my baby sister as we waited in town. It was crowded, and we were near a fresh food marketplace. We were excited to see my dad, who had been away working in faraway lands. I was overcome with joy when I saw him on the other side of the town square. I could see the excitement on his face. I remember what he was wearing: quarter-length khaki shorts, a thinly striped shirt with rolled sleeves, and an old-fashioned cap. Excited, I let go of my mother's hand and ran towards my papa.

In my eagerness to hug my papa, I didn't see the horse and carriage traveling at speed, which ran right over me. My leg was broken, and my knees were severely damaged. I also had severe brain damage, which made it a challenge to look after me. My family was poor, and I was too much for everyone. I had become a vegetable and a burden on my family. My grandad couldn't stand to see me suffer any longer, and he suffocated me with a pillow. Reliving this lifetime, I accepted this was how it was meant to be. I felt little or no sorrow, just an understanding that everyone in our life plays their part in giving us the experiences we need to evolve.

Our wounds are here to serve us, allowing us to have empathy with other people's circumstances. When we do this, we realize that we are all equal emotionally. Every human being on this planet has something they are afraid of, some disappointment. Everyone has had a broken heart. The more we realize this, the easier it becomes to connect with others. Healing is an attitude of understanding that everything happens because our lives matter and are for the greater good. Being a breathing, living human being is enough. You are enough.

Shaking Or Not Shaking: That Is The Question

I received one of the most profound healings in Bali in 2013 at a shaking ashram. I didn't even know that I needed healing as, at this point, I had already completed many courses and programs. Following my intuition, I went along after finishing a six-month contract teaching NLP in Singapore for a training company based in Bali. While living in Sydney, I had read about the ashram's leader in a spiritual magazine. I didn't know why, but I immediately thought I would like to attend one of his retreats. I rocked up at the retreat with an open mind and made a pact with myself that I would stick out the five days, no matter how woo-woo things got.

The agenda for the shaking was pretty simple. The day would begin with two hours of shaking before breakfast, two hours before lunch, and then two hours before dinner.

I arrived Saturday afternoon just in time for the evening shaking session, having no idea what I was getting into. None whatsoever. I had never shaken before. I didn't even know if I was doing it correctly. The first session was the hardest both from a physical point of view and mentally, too, because I felt so stupid standing there, shaking. I felt like I was doing it wrong. It was tough to let go of the mind and go with the flow. Everyone seemed weird and so different from me. People were laughing for no reason while shaking, and it felt like they were laughing at me.

Later that night, I was having a quiet moment of reflection when one of the experienced shakers came over and asked if everything was okay. She must have sensed that I was thinking of quitting. She explained to me that her first time had been trying for her as well. We went through a mini-shaking workshop on how to shake properly. It was so helpful. Things were looking better.

Then, I met my roommate, who had been shaking for some time in the UK. Although this was his first shaking retreat, he had already been at the ashram for three weeks. He explained the whole ritual to me, and he guided me through it. The first session of the day started at 7 a.m., and he told me that they shot a syringe full of blessed liquid tobacco up each nostril and one squirt orally. I couldn't believe what I was hearing. I made a pact with myself to go through with it, but this sounded crazy. I decided to wait until the morning to make a decision.

My roomy had set his alarm so we would arrive at the shaking hall early. People were already there, coughing and splattering all over the place. Unfazed, my roommate filled his syringe full of liquid tobacco, held it in front of himself, imagined seeing a white light, and then squirted up the nostril. After he had completed the whole process, it was my turn. I half-filled the syringe, imagined it as white light, and squirted it up one nostril. Instantly, I felt a warm sensation in my third eye chakra. To my surprise, it wasn't bad at all. I repeated the same process for the other nostril, and I drank a syringe full as well. Orally, it was disgusting. But I was determined to stomach it. I drank a few mouthfuls of water to wash it down. Feeling good to go, we entered the hall and sat on the timber floor, ready to sing the Gayatri mantra. It's composed in Sanskrit, and I had no idea what it meant then, but I felt positive vibes while singing it. Later, I discovered it is one of the oldest known mantras. The English translation is as follows.

Om: The primeval sound. **Bhur**: The physical body/physical realm. **Bhuvah**: The life force/the mental realm. **Suvah**: The soul/spiritual realm. **Tat**: That (God). **Savitur**: The Sun, Creator (source of all life). **Vareñyam**: Adore. **Bhargo**: Effulgence (divine light). **Devasya**: Supreme Lord. **Dhīmahi**: Meditate. **Dhiyo**: The intellect. **Yo**: May this light. **No**: Our. **Prachodayāt**: Illumine/inspire.

Om Bhur Bhuvaḥ Swaḥ
Tat-savitur Vareñyaṃ
Bhargo Devasya Dhīmahi
Dhiyo Yonaḥ Prachodayāt

The first shaking session of the day was still a little bit of a challenge. It was a bit difficult to find my rhythm, but it was an improvement on the night before. The session before lunch was enjoyable. It almost felt like benevolent forces were shaking me. I felt a stream of energy centers open up above my head. It felt like an electric current of some sort. It was an intense feeling. And then, seemingly out of nowhere, came Ratu Bagus, the spiritual guru running the ashram. He came around to my right, stepped on my foot, and said in a funny voice, "Electric, electric, electric." My entire body started to shake violently. To anyone watching, I'm sure it looked like my head and neck would come off my shoulders—the shaking was that insane.

All of a sudden, Ratu took his foot off mine. I was completely losing control of my feet, slipping and sliding everywhere. Eventually, I fell over with an almighty smack. My head cracked the tile floor so hard that everyone awaited my reaction. The people who had been laughing at me before now looked worried. I finally got up, not feeling any pain and laughing uncontrollably. There was no lump or feeling of any pain whatsoever. I was now a believer in shaking.

I witnessed many similar events over my five days. One that stood out the most was on one of the evenings when a muscly-looking guy wasn't really getting into the sessions and was being entirely negative. His thoughts were so loud that we could all hear them. At the end of each evening session, Ratu would call a few people to the front of the room to demonstrate his power. He called the big Dutch guy out. An alpha male type with muscles on muscles, he could have even been a bodybuilder. The guy walked straight over to the guru and folded his arms in his face. He was wearing an angry look.

Ratu quietly stepped backward and laughed while stroking his goatee. Being short, with his long white hair tied in a ponytail, Ratu had to reach up to place his hand on the Dutchie's shoulder. The big Dutchman's facial expression changed to one of surprise. He began to move involuntarily. Ratu removed his hand. Then, WOW! Big Dutchie started bouncing across the room like he was on a pogo stick, still with his arms crossed, bouncing straight into a concrete pole and falling to the floor. It was so funny. Everyone laughed as his arms were again crossed, and his legs moved as if he was still bouncing upright on a pogo stick.

At this point, you either think this is unbelievable or ask yourself what healing I had received from what this woo-woo retreat was. At the end of the third day, to my disbelief, I noticed an inch-long ulcer in my mouth. I've had plenty of mouth sores before, but they are usually pinhead-sized and sting a little. After some sea salt, they vanish in two to three days, right? This one was huge. I showed my roomy, and he was almost excited and told me to put some dry holy tobacco on it. After everything I had experienced and witnessed, I thought, Why not? Even though I'm generally not a fan of tobacco or smoking. With my mouth full of tobacco, I felt like John Wayne spitting tobacco juice. It was gross. I looked in the mirror the following day, and the ulcer was gone. Nada. Nothing. I couldn't believe what I was seeing.

I received the subsequent healing on the second to last day after lunch. I was shaking away effortlessly, feeling the presence of divine beings, and breaking into the occasional fit of laughter when I started to feel intense, sharp pain in my heart, almost like a mini heart attack. My intuition told me to keep shaking and laugh it out. The sensation lasted virtually the entire session, dissipating, and then subsiding completely. I felt utterly present. Walking out of the shaking hall, my body began to tingle all over, and I felt my spirit leave my body and then re-enter. As my spirit re-entered, my entire body was shaking. My roomy came to my aid, putting me into the shower. As I was feeling extremely vulnerable, he walked with me to the lunchroom and assured me that all I needed to do was ground my body with some food.

Upon reflection and meditation, I concluded that my molecular structure had been transformed, healing my broken heart from my childhood, and clearing out any hereditary heart conditions as well. Some 13 years earlier, I had been suffering from anxiety attacks and pains in my heart. After running a series of tests, the doctor told me I had heart murmurs. He gave me some medication to take, and that was it. My dad has had many heart attacks and had a pacemaker to help his heartbeat. Since my experience with Ratu, my heart feels as strong as an ox. When my five days at the shaking retreat were up, I decided to climb Mt. Agung, a nearby volcano, and my levels of consciousness were incredibly heightened for three days afterward. Those three days were so blissful.

In pursuing the development of spirit-full leadership skills, consider seeking the guidance of a Reiki master, engaging in a regular yoga practice, participating in meditation classes, or embracing a retreat focused on your personal growth. Recognizing our blind spots and venturing beyond our comfort zones is transformative. I have found immense fulfillment in delving into the depths of my own identity. The path of healing is an odyssey filled with discovery and adventure, and true freedom lies in living unburdened by emotional constraints.

"A true spirit-full leader leads by example, embodying the values and principals they espouse."

~ Unknown

Energy

We are energy!

We are spiritual beings, we are energy beings, everything is energy, and we are everything.

The only thing energy wants is to move around, manifest, change, transform, and, most importantly, expand. This is not religion, politics, or beliefs; this is pure physics.

First, there is energy, then there is matter. The energy that has come into life, such as humans.

Humans have been given a great gift: consciousness. We have the ability to consciously understand the physics of the universe and the remarkable gift of deliberately turning energy into matter and transforming matter into other types of energy. Using the universe's creative force to innovate and create things for our benefit is helpful. We are the only species known to men that have that gift. So, we need to be aware of how we use our gifts.

Our mind and memory systems have evolved so much that we can benefit from earlier experiences to design new, more sophisticated things.

Like information technology and artificial intelligence, which are replicas of our gift to process information and learn from our actions, knowledge downloaded from a virtual dimension has been manifested in technology by humans.

If you zoom out enough, you need not be a scientist to understand this. Wise men and women have known this for ages; science has made us expand our awareness and find proof to more sophisticated levels. We need to be curious and spend time looking around the corner without bringing with us any limitations and beliefs.

The first time I remember reflecting on the energy thing was when I was a little boy. I could not understand why older people argued, fought about unimportant things, and made a mess. As a child, I did not know what all of this was, but still, I knew in some way. It made me feel bad. Other times, it was so easy; everyone was happy. Could we not just choose the happy place? After all, we are here to play and have a good time together, aren't we? At least, that was the kid's idea of life.

I could feel their energy and sense their thoughts; I saw things like shadows, which made me feel uncomfortable. Without knowing, I knew that it was energy. While expressing this, the grown-up world did not take it in, saying it is not real. This is something that I have been confronting my whole life: that what I sense, see, know, that others do not perceive, see, or know is not considered authentic. This early sensitivity to energy was one of the experiences that laid the foundation for my later understanding of leadership as an energy-guided endeavor.

These personal insights echo in the realm of quantum physics. Through their curiosity, great scientists have put words and understanding into complex parts of reality.

Alain Aspect, John Clauser, and Anton Zeilinger won the Nobel Prize in Physics in 2022 for their experiments with quantum particles in entangled states. The Nobel Prize website says, "What happens to one particle in an entangled pair determines what happens to the other, even if they are too far apart to affect each other. The laureates' development of experimental tools has laid the foundation for a new era of quantum technology."

Science has proven that the interconnectedness observed in quantum particles mirrors the interconnectedness in human interactions and leadership, where energy and consciousness play a pivotal role. By this, we can say that it is also a fact that things are happening beyond our knowing and understanding, so let's stop neglecting those who see more, feel more, and know more than others. It might just be someone curious and able to look around the corner into the unknown. Perhaps what that person sees will be acknowledged as science one day.

Energy as a navigator

Humans have a built-in energy sensory system; our energy fields are connected to our senses and feelings. Our feelings are a navigation tool designed to help us survive and thrive on Earth. This sophisticated system was developed millions of years before our brains were developed to the current level. Though, in our modern society we underestimate the feeling and sensory systems and see them as less effective than our minds.

The energy field extends far beyond our body, and highly sensitive people can feel energy from miles away, even from another part of the world.

Energy

Feelings are the translation toolkit between spirit and body. They are the language of the soul, and we usually express them through colors, poetry, art, and visions.

The system that was first designed to make us survive nowadays appears to kidnap humans in everyday activities and situations. This is the human drama we call society.

When we wake up and become observers of our feelings and thoughts, we can use the navigation toolbox for what it was designed for. To know if we should go right or left, we can choose what's good for us or bad for us.

Every feeling has its frequency, vibration, or energy, whatever we want to call it. So, we can tune into love and experience it without a lover on our side. It's not a feeling, it's not an activity, it's a frequency. We can tune into anger, experience it, and learn what it wants to tell us for our step-by-step navigation.

When, for instance, we live the true energy of love, we will start to experience and live a reality based on love. The more we build our relationship with that frequency, the more natural that will be to us, and the more we will recognize it in others and reality.

Sometimes, we say that we live out of survival values; my perception is that survival is a fundamental energy to us, just as reproduction, which is an expression of the creative force of the universe. All species want to reproduce, just as energy wants to move around and reproduce itself. So, in some way, survival is a basis for living, though when we evolve, other energies expand. Survival is a sense of the infinite life force that wants to continue experiencing what it is to be a human in your body.

What has this to do with leadership?

If we can't sense our own and other's feelings (energies) and observe this, the efficiency of our leadership sensory system decreases rapidly to deficient and primitive levels. We get stuck in our minds and our own beliefs. So, there is a massive potential that we as leaders do not reach since we do not develop our ability to be energy beings.

The ability to sense and understand our emotions and those of others is crucial in leadership. For instance, a leader who can empathize with their team's stress before a project's deadline can adjust strategies to maintain morale and productivity. Another example is the typical merger of businesses where different cultures and ways of cooperation should become one new way. To sense exactly where and what the tension is, and, with patience, we must adjust how we act and navigate to bring harmony might be the difference between success and disaster. This energy awareness transforms leadership from mere management to a more empathetic and effective practice.

Let's take frustration and satisfaction as an example. These are our two feelings and body sensations, our greatest navigation tools.

Frustration tells us, "I don't like or should avoid this." It also tells us that something is blocking our way, and we should spend much time investigating and processing it. Satisfaction tells us, "Oh, I like this, I want more of this, this is good."

Like go left or go right. It is straightforward and not complicated if we do not avoid our feelings or other's feelings. When we enter the stage that my feeling is right, yours is wrong, then shit hits the fan, and the human drama is in our face.

The problem is that today's leaders are undereducated. They are good at the "thing," like economics, marketing, technology, and management, but they suck at leadership. They suck at being in tune with their navigation toolkit and their soul.

Why?

They have not learned what it means to be a fellow human being; thus, they are not leaders. They are merely managers who, in the best case, have learned management. And, by far, this is only getting worse since today, we only hunt for more short-term results, money, and power, but not real sustainable growth. We lack patience. That's why we can wonder whether our evolution in the present is going forward or backward; only history will tell.

Business schools do not teach this to leaders, schools do not teach it, and parents do not teach it; why? Because so few know it is crucial to personal success.

Managers have not learned the basic mechanics of how a human works because they have not done their personal development and have never been taught how to do it. We spend an awful amount of time learning technical theories, math, and religion, but we spend very little time learning about ourselves. Thus, we will remain undereducated in this field. The only way to understand this is to do our job ourselves, to experience it. Everything starts and finishes with us.

By this, we don't know and are unaware of the hidden super potential waiting to unfold.

The solution is to let our inner observer embrace what we feel, love our feelings, play with them, relate to them, and ask them what they want to tell us. And then do a reality check. Is that true? Since feelings are sometimes chemical reactions, we shall not do anything until the storm inside has settled. If in total anger, hate, or discernment, brew yourself a cup of tea and enjoy that blissful moment.

Since managers are undereducated, most companies become victims of people's feelings and thoughts. They lose the opportunity to explore and utilize their potential and stay stuck in whatever illusion the management lives by.

You do not learn this by reading a book, taking a three-day leadership course, or attending university. Sorry, but plenty of leadership courses teach nothing and are expensive; leadership is not theory; leadership is being. A short course could give a glimpse of what is possible, but they do not teach, even though it could be a start, and even become an eye-opener.

You learn about energy and leadership by getting a mentor who has made the journey themselves; that's why modern society fails to educate leaders, real leaders. Society believes that everything should be taught in a classroom by teachers who have learned theory but not necessarily done the inner work. We also suffer from the I can manage myself attitude, which is blindness; we are never self-made. No one learns anything by themselves; we are always influenced by someone, even when we invent something completely new. As I have described in this book, I have personally experienced that.

The teacher should have walked deeper into the forest than you have, deep into the experience, so that the teacher can help you navigate this passage if you get lost. A coach training program, or a certified education is not proof that a person has done their inner work. It just means they have passed an exam, even if it is from a highly-ranked business school. I learned most of my greatest leadership skills from people who were not from the business world at all. They were people who had made their journey to find expanded consciousness and learned what it is to be a fellow human being who had seen the deep connection to the heart.

So, feelings are a navigation toolkit and nothing to be kidnapped by or be afraid of, not our own and not others. On the contrary, they sit on a massive load of information on how we should handle the situation and what the situation wants to tell us.

Feelings are more trustworthy than our thoughts since our mind is a toolbox that does what we tell it to do. Our mind can innovate atomic bombs, create a new medicine that heals sickness, or make a water purifier. If our energy level is stuck on anger, hate, and revenge, we might be able to innovate something that could kill our opponent, and our minds will make it happen. Our mind is an effective machine, like a computer.

Energetic feedback

We always get feedback instantly, like when I pressed the keyboard when writing this. From somewhere came the idea to write this; it traveled through my system, came out through my fingers which then touched the keyboard, and immediately, I got the feedback. I felt the keyboard under my fingertips and got feedback that I could read this text.

If I sit in a chair, I get the feedback that the chair supports me, the house keeps the chair, the Earth supports the house, and the universe supports the Earth, and instantly, we get the feedback from the universe that we are supported. We are always backed by gravity since if there were no gravity, we would be thrown off this planet and into infinity, and so would everything loose on this Earth since we are spinning at 30.000 km/h.

We live in a system with opposing forces and polarities; without them, the Earth would not work. We have a north pole and a south pole; we have good and bad; we have cold and warm. Our complete existence is of opposing forces, as are we humans. We have, though, been given consciousness to navigate this world of polarity, and we are supposed to use it to our benefit; why else should we have been given it?

There is this continuous wave or wind of energy which we can sail on, where we always get feedback or response from reality, from the energy. From a leadership perspective, it can be seen and experienced as a response from the humans that follow or do not follow our ways of influencing them, with what energy they follow or obey because they must.

From a spirit-full leadership standpoint, acknowledging free will is paramount. If we influence someone and they follow by their free will, they will do it with a big YES and be aware of what they do! If they do it with not-so-free will, fear is at play, and they will either do it half-heartedly because they think they must do it to survive, to fit in, or to be someone. Or at least that is what our human system says it must do.

Leadership involves consciousness and higher frequency levels, which means energy. In this case, it's not being a dopamine kicker. But leadership as a being of gratitude, love, empathy, and compassion is high-frequency levels of energy, which, if we start to embody them, integrate them into ourselves, we begin to emit them, it will affect our behavior, the way we talk, what we say, what we do, what we give our attention to, focus on, who we associate with, what we eat and what we consume.

The Power of Numbers

There is a power in numbers, which means the amount of energy and mass, i.e., gravity, accumulates into a significant number. A practical example is that if many say we will have a recession, we surely will. When the mighty, with a lot of influence, say it, we will have it. Groupthink accelerates circumstances in directions that we manifest. We predict our future by the energy we send into it. That's why the future does not come toward us; we call for it and create it in every moment.

Books have already been written about the mastermind, the force and persona created when a group comes together, which represents the power of numbers. A mastermind can be productive or destructive, depending on which energies it sources from. Sourcing strategies can be applied to energy, not only to traditional management strategies but also to where we get our resources.

Eight billion people on Earth form a massive mastermind, unaware that it is a mastermind, eight billion minds, thoughts, and feelings that create human destiny. Earth does not care; Earth will reshape, reframe, and continue; she only responds to what we do.

The mastermind is pure math; one brilliant man can easily be outnumbered by several less intelligent people who unite in a group. Also, brutality coming together as a mastermind is devastating; history is full of examples. Brilliant master minds are never brutal or greedy; neither are true spirit-full leaders. They cannot harm; it would be going against their energy.

A spirit-full leader must develop a strong heart and mind. This leadership influences people to follow, creating new masterminds.

I experienced this when I was working in the political field, and it did not matter how brilliant the work presented by the organization was if the council of politicians did not like it or did not understand it. So many times, we did not come further than what the mastermind allowed to happen. We changed our way of working to process the awareness of a question, or subject. With the council (mastermind) our focus is to increase the awareness of the issues in the council, helping them to brilliance, not showing off our own. We gained ground faster, and the decision-making was more long-term and sustainable. Before that, it was easy to gain trust for a cause in a small group, but when it came to a bigger group of people, suddenly, something happened. This shows the power of the mastermind, which equals the power of numbers.

As a spirit-full leader, you need to know how to lead. You are not the leader; and you are the follower. The energy from the frequency that wants to be created leads, and we should listen to it—not mistaken to be the minds of the people in the organization. The energy might be communicated through the people, but it is always the energy that wants to be created that leads. So, listen to the energy and know you have the power to direct it.

When we act out of our hearts and follow the energy of the good that wants to be created, that good will be strong; remember, a war never lasts; peace is superior. It always is, and peace is the only thing we can stand in the long run. Everything else suffocates us.

As mentioned above, a group can easily outnumber one person; many times in movies, the hero outnumbers a big group. Well, that can be done, and we also have stories about small, strong groups that have defeated larger forces. The reason is desire or faith, better education, training, and structure; either we win, or we die, so we better win.

But when this comes to ordinary circumstances, other forces are at play. The change comes when it is ready and supposed to; if we try to speed up or force the change to happen, we will probably only create tension or protest. Tension is the natural signal that needs to be listened to since tension seeks its resolution.

You might have a great idea and be quite brilliant, but the idea is so challenging that it meets tons of energy blocks of fear. To succeed, it either needs to be a systemic change, like introducing smartphones, which have drastically changed behavior, or it needs to answer a need from the masses if that idea should have a chance to last beyond your presence.

We want change, but we do not want to be changed.

One man can be so brilliant and intense that he can motivate a big change, but even he can be defeated by other forces that prevent change from happening. If there is no match between that person, the cause, and the organization, it might not be the right time, or the opposing forces are too strong. I think history is full of examples, like Martin Luther King and Dag Hammarskjöld, to name a couple.

Sometimes, the spirit-full leader needs to understand that the situation or the timing is incorrect, and then you must either accept the situation, change, or leave the situation.

Energy Cycles

Everything works in cycles, which means in frequency waves, and there are universal laws that define that, which physics can describe much better than we can.

However, the real interesting thing about humans and energy cycles is which cycles we have let define our way of living, structuring our societies, our schools, and our workplaces. In a great deal of the world, societies have been structured around how men function as human beings and not about how women function as human beings. In many societies, work schedules, leadership models, and even urban planning have traditionally been designed with male patterns in mind, often neglecting female health cycles, caregiving responsibilities, and work-life balance needs. I have often wondered what the world would have looked like if it had been designed based on women's functioning and cycles. Perhaps society would be more flexible, dynamic, spatial, and democratic. After all, very few things work naturally according to an assembly line and lean production.

Since the Industrial Revolution, people have been treated like machines, like humanbots. We go to work at seven a.m. and go home at four p.m., or nine to five, or work many more hours a week,

60, 70, 80 for many managers and workers. Today, it's five or six days a week; earlier, it was every day of the week.

With the Industrial Revolution, mankind has lost its connection with natural rhythms, its connection with nature, and even natural cycles. Even farming has become industrialized, which does not consider natural circumstances. For instance, crops can be grown in places not suited for them by pumping water from underground sources called aqua spheres, just like we pump oil. These are pockets of water that, when empty, will not fill up again for thousands of years. This is an example of mankind that has lost its connection to nature and natural cycles and become humanbots.

The Industrial Revolution has led to a lot of progress, health, wealth, and innovation, and a lot more equality. Still, it also led to us losing connection to one of our greatest gifts, the connection to our true nature, the rhythm of our soul, and the rhythm of nature. To function in that society, we had to close off our connection to our feelings and emotions, and we did that to survive, and we still do it to survive, but now many of us have forgotten that. We just run in the hamster wheel because that has become the norm, and we do not know that it could be different. Especially in the last 10 – 20 years, society has become speed-blinded by a growth mindset, and the urge for more and more at any cost has increased exponentially. Even the climate problem has made us blind; we believe it's about negotiation and boosting our fears. It's not; it's a wake-up call our mother sent us when she saw that mankind ran off in the wrong direction, forgetting who we are.

Of course, we cannot go back; we never can; we can only go forward and act in the present moment. So, we need to find a way to reconnect with nature and our nature and to start living in harmony with nature in a modern way in a globalized world. This could involve inner development practices in schools and universities that promote reconnection with nature, like meditation in nature, tree-hugging, or eating more natural foods. It could also include integrating green spaces into urban design, promoting flexible work hours to align more closely with natural human rhythms, and encouraging sustainable practices at individual and corporate levels.

There is an urge for a massive systemic shift in leadership. More leaders need to follow the voice of the spirit and be in tune with nature and the greater good, not only letting everything be ruled by economics. Ultimately, we must realize that what is good for the Earth is the priority, not what is good for mankind or the individual. A massive realization that is hard to take in and even harder to start living by. We are a spendable species; Earth does not need us; we need Earth and have been given it as a playground.

However, there is hope that we will crack the code to new levels of consciousness.

Richness is a Quality of Being

The soul's language is pure frequencies, the pure energies. We can feel them in our bodies, and it's how the spirit communicates with our bodies and minds. Chemical and electrical signals run through our bodies, and our energy field sensors everything and everyone around us.

Richness is a quality of being an experience of expanding pure frequencies. This follows the law of resonance.

When we resonate from pure frequencies such as love, joy, happiness, empathy, and compassion without attachment to our thoughts, mind, and beliefs, our reference system accurately sends and responds to equal frequencies from others from existence.

We all know this from the saying, "Smile, and the world smiles back on you." This is an example of the mirror neurons in the human system. When we see someone smile, our neurons are programmed to smile back. That's why a baby smiles back when it sees their parent smile at them.

When we cultivate a being of richness in pure frequencies, the world around us will respond by acknowledging that, and maybe even give you feedback.

We get love back when we cultivate, emit, and express love.

We come to this world as a child but are planted as a seed. This seed would continue to be a seed and not become a child if we were not programmed to develop and grow. Develop and grow until we flower; from that, we continue to grow and flower. The big game changer is if we awaken and become aware of the mechanics and laws that make us grow and continue to wake up more and more during our growth journey, then we can expand consciously more and more. There is no stop for our growth, for our journey to richness.

Spirit-full leaders know how to grow richness as a quality of being, consciously or unconsciously, to be a good fellow human being. They know the importance of getting to know themselves to understand the human system. They put themselves into experiences that make them grow, and they have practices that make them grow, like meditation. They connect with nature to know their nature and grow their respect and gratitude for the Earth that nurtures them, like Dag Hammarskjöld, who has chosen solitude and hiking in the wilderness of the Swedish north in the summertime. And most importantly, they do not get lost in the fast lane of modern society.

To put it bluntly and honestly, the spirit-full leader grows a character and an energy that makes them great people, great fellow human beings. They grow more honest, tolerant, loving, and even brave.

A true spirit-full leader will become a role model, influencing their peers through their presence. Their character is natural, and they have a strong presence.

They emit this energy, shine their light upon things; they hold space. Not so much by what they do but by who they are. Their actions and decisions will show a way.

To grow this quality of being, choosing your role models carefully and choosing whom you learn from is important. Remember that anybody can heal; be careful who you choose to heal you. Being a dopamine kicker does not help anyone to awaken, and drugs do not allow anyone to awaken.

Many say there is no such thing as right and wrong, but from a universal perspective, from existence, there seems to be a recipe for right and wrong: right is sustainable, and wrong is destructive. There have already been people walking on Earth who have uncovered this for us; the rest of us could only cultivate the gifts they have left behind. Still, many choose not to open up to the wisdom they have left behind.

History is full of those who have chosen to walk the path, but it is even more full of those who have not. When we write history, we write about the violent men who conquered with primitive and low-level energies. Humanity is still licking its wounds from history's mistakes and repeating them repeatedly. It's time to make a change and to co-create life on this planet for the good of Earth and all species, including humankind.

It's time to cultivate the character of natural richness to make it a quality of being.

"The role of a great leader is not to give greatness to human beings, but to help them extract greatness they already have inside them."

~ J. Buchan

Cultivating Insights and Wisdom

W e live in a world where integrity, interpersonal relationships, and wholeness connect us to the core. We aim to protect and build, to love and respect our community, and to lead our people into an illuminated world where our spirit is free yet well-connected.

A leader must have a specific set of spiritual beliefs to earn the trust of those who follow them. After all, we are spiritual beings going through a human experience, so if we follow someone or expect someone to believe in us, we want to be able to connect with them. The insights and what we stand for can act as a point of connection with others.

We tend to focus a lot on the beliefs that connect us to the human experience but less on the wisdom that ties us to our spiritual experience. Yet, insights are of great importance when forming a connection. The more grounded a spiritual leader is with the wisdom and insights they possess, the more their effectiveness as leaders increases.

Insights and wisdom should not be confused with one another; insights are new understandings that are observed and experienced. Insights allow us to see the wisdom in the knowledge at hand. They can be gained through analysis, observation, or a sudden realization, providing a deeper understanding of a particular aspect.

Wisdom is a broader and more encompassing concept. It involves the ability to make sound judgments and decisions based on knowledge, experience, and a deep understanding of life. Wisdom often goes beyond specific situations and encompasses a more comprehensive view of life and its complexities.

Insights are specific moments of clarity or understanding. At the same time, wisdom is a more comprehensive and overarching quality that involves the application of knowledge and insights to make judicious decisions and lead a meaningful life. Wisdom often comes with experience and a broader perspective on life's complexities.

Combining wisdom and insights yields a powerful synergy that enhances one's ability to navigate life's challenges and make informed decisions. Insights provide the depth of understanding necessary to grasp specific situations, unravel complexities, and uncover profound truths. On the other hand, wisdom brings a broader perspective, integrating these insights into a comprehensive framework that considers the larger context of life.

Together, they form a dynamic duo that equips leaders with the knowledge to address immediate issues and empowers them to make sound, far-sighted decisions. This combination fosters a holistic approach to life, applying learned lessons and cultivating a discerning and balanced approach to challenges.

This chapter delves into the significance of insights and wisdom, exploring how spirit-full leaders, imbued with a spirit-driven ethos, harness these qualities to become truly inspirational figures. The integration of insights and wisdom, coupled with the solid values of a spirit-full leader, broadens the collective mindset, fortifies the team's physical and emotional dimensions, and nurtures a profound sense of interconnectedness. Together, these elements contribute to cultivating a holistic perspective that encompasses the mind, body, heart, and spirit, ultimately fostering a unified and harmonious approach within the team.

The Journey

The journey of spirit-full leaders toward gaining insights and wisdom is a multifaceted and dynamic process, intricately woven with personal development, experiences, and a deep connection to a guiding ethos. These leaders embark on a continuous quest for understanding, driven by a commitment to self-discovery and the well-being of those they lead.

At the core of this journey is a profound self-awareness that spirit-full leaders cultivate. They engage in introspection, examining their values, strengths, and weaknesses. Through this process, they gain insights into their own motivations and convictions, laying the foundation for authentic leadership. This self-awareness serves as a compass, guiding them in aligning their actions with their core values and principles.

Spirit-full leaders actively seek diverse perspectives and experiences to broaden their understanding of the world. They embrace a continuous learning mindset, acknowledging that wisdom often emerges from synthesizing various viewpoints. This commitment to lifelong learning positions them to adapt to changing circumstances and challenges, fostering resilience and agility.

A crucial aspect of gaining insights and wisdom for spirit-full leaders is the practice of mindfulness. They cultivate the ability to be fully present in the moment, attuning themselves to the needs and nuances of their surroundings. Mindfulness allows them to observe, listen, and empathize, leading to a deeper understanding of the people they serve and the context in which they operate.

In the pursuit of wisdom, spirit-full leaders often turn to mentorship and guidance from those who have walked similar paths. Mentors provide not only practical advice but also share the wisdom born of their own experiences. Through these relationships, leaders gain valuable insights that transcend theoretical knowledge, offering practical applications rooted in real-world scenarios.

Integrating spiritual principles and values forms a cornerstone of the journey toward wisdom for spirit-full leaders. Whether grounded in religious faith, philosophical beliefs, or a sense of interconnectedness with the universe, these leaders draw upon spiritual foundations to guide their decision-making and actions. This spiritual grounding fosters a sense of purpose and direction, contributing to developing a wise and centered leadership style.

Spirit-full leaders recognize the importance of humility in their quest for wisdom. They acknowledge that true understanding is a lifelong pursuit and do not have all the answers. This humility opens the door to continuous growth and learning as they remain open to new ideas, perspectives, and ways of approaching challenges.

Cultivating emotional intelligence is another key aspect of the journey toward wisdom for spirit-full leaders. They understand the profound impact of emotions on decision-making and interpersonal relationships. By honing their emotional intelligence, these leaders navigate complex social dynamics with empathy and insight, fostering harmonious and productive relationships within their teams.

Reflective practices, such as journaling and contemplation, are pivotal in developing insights and wisdom for spirit-full leaders. These leaders set aside dedicated time for introspection, allowing them to process their experiences, discern patterns, and extract meaningful lessons. Through reflection, they gain clarity on their values, refine their leadership approach, and continually evolve as humans.

Spirit-full leaders often acknowledge the connection between nature and wisdom. Immersing themselves in natural environments provides a space for contemplation and renewal. Nature serves as a source of inspiration and a reminder of the interconnectedness of all living things. Through this connection, leaders gain insights into the cyclical nature of challenges and the importance of adaptability in leadership.

The journey of spirit-full leaders toward gaining insights and wisdom is a holistic and continuous process that encompasses self-awareness, learning, mindfulness, mentorship, spirituality, humility, emotional intelligence, and reflective practices. These leaders recognize that wisdom is not a destination but a dynamic and evolving state of being. By embracing these elements, spirit-full leaders enhance their leadership capabilities and create a positive and transformative impact on the individuals and organizations they lead.

"A Spirit-full leader serves as a guiding light, helping others find their way in the darkness and navigate life's challenges."

~ Unknown

Nurturing Spirit-Full Leadership through Mentorship: Cultivating Insights, Wisdom, and Practical Applications

―――――――∾∾∾――――――――

S pirit-full leadership is a holistic approach that transcends conventional management styles, drawing inspiration from a deep well of insights and wisdom. Within this paradigm, mentors become not only instrumental but sacred—a guiding force that nurtures the spiritual essence of leadership. The transformative role of mentors in developing spirit-full leaders cannot be overstated.

Mentorship in spirit-full leadership goes beyond the traditional transfer of skills; it involves the cultivation of a profound inner understanding. Mentors, often seasoned leaders themselves, serve as spiritual guides, helping mentees explore the depths of their own consciousness. Through introspective conversations and guided reflections, mentors facilitate a journey of self-discovery, allowing emerging leaders to tap into their own wellspring of insights.

The mentor becomes a beacon of wisdom, sharing practical knowledge and timeless truths that resonate with the spirit-full leader's quest for meaning. In this context, wisdom is not a mere accumulation of facts; it is a deep understanding of the underlying principles that govern leadership with authenticity and purpose. The mentor imparts wisdom by encouraging contemplation, introspection, and aligning actions with spiritual principles, fostering an insightful and wise leadership style.

Mentorship in spirit-full leadership often involves storytelling, a powerful means of transferring knowledge and the essence of lived experiences. Mentees absorb the nuances of the mentor's journey, gaining insights into the challenges and joys of leadership from a spiritual perspective.

The mentorship relationship bridges generations of spirit-full leaders, fostering a continuum of spiritual insights. As mentees navigate their own leadership challenges, they draw upon the collective wisdom of those who walked the path before them. The mentor's experiences serve as beacons, illuminating the way and providing a spiritual compass for the mentee's own leadership journey.

One of the practical applications of mentorship insights is in the art of conscious decision-making. Spirit-full leaders, guided by their mentors, learn to make decisions that align with their spiritual values and principles. This conscious decision-making process goes beyond a utilitarian analysis of pros and cons; it involves a deep consideration of the impact on the self, others, and the collective spirit of the organization.

Communication in spirit-full leadership becomes a sacred exchange of ideas guided by the principles of empathy and understanding. Mentors impart the art of mindful communication, emphasizing the importance of listening deeply, expressing authentically, and fostering mutual respect. The practical application of these communication insights creates a culture of open dialogue and genuine connection within the organization.

Furthermore, the mentorship journey contributes significantly to the development of emotional intelligence in spirit-full leaders.

Embracing the mentor's insights on navigating the emotional landscape of leadership, mentees learn to lead with compassion, respond with equanimity, and cultivate a harmonious workplace environment. The practical application of emotional intelligence insights in spirit-full leadership fosters a culture where the emotional well-being of individuals is honored and considered an integral part of organizational success.

In the dance of spirit-full leadership, mentors are the custodians of ancient wisdom, passing the torch to the next generation of leaders. The mentorship relationship becomes a pilgrimage, a journey where insights are not just intellectual understandings but revelations that touch the soul. Cultivating insights and wisdom under the guidance of a mentor is a transformative process that shapes effective leaders and stewards of a higher purpose.

As spirit-full leaders navigate their mentorship journey, they emerge with practical skills and a profound understanding of the spiritual dimensions of leadership. The insights and wisdom gained through mentorship become the guiding stars, illuminating the path toward leadership that is effective, deeply meaningful, and spiritually resonant. In this sacred journey of mentorship, spirit-full leaders find guides and kindred spirits who illuminate the way with the eternal flame of wisdom.

"Leadership is based on inspiration, not domination; cooperation, not intimidation."

~ Wiliam Arthur Wood

The Discerning Eye

A spirit-full leader possesses a discerning eye that transcends the ordinary perception of the world. Such leaders are not merely perceptive; they are intelligent and insightful and can grasp the deeper truths that elude others. In Martin Luther King Jr.'s spirit-full leadership, this discernment extended beyond the superficial boundaries of race, color, or beliefs. His visionary perception of reality led him to treat every human being as equal, embodying the essence of spirit-full leadership.

King's profound understanding, articulated in his iconic "I Have a Dream" speech, envisioned a world where judgment was based not on external attributes but on a person's intrinsic character and values. His discerning eye saw past surface differences, recognizing the shared spiritual experience uniting humanity. This intuitive perception is a foundation for fostering innate wisdom for a spirit-full leader like King.

The concept of intuition, often synonymous with perceptive abilities, takes on a deeper meaning in the realm of spirit-full leadership. A leader with a discerning eye, guided by intuition, can perceive shifts in attitudes, identify allies, and discern potential threats. This heightened awareness allows them to navigate challenges profoundly, avoid surprises, and make informed decisions. In the spirit-full leader's quest for insights and wisdom, intuition becomes a guiding force that aligns with the universal flow of spiritual energy.

Spirit-full leaders, akin to Reverend Michael Beckwith, exemplify the transformative power of a discerning eye in personal awakening. Beckwith's early struggles and spiritual resistance eventually gave way to a heightened perception that others might have overlooked. Through a recurring dream that symbolized a spiritual death and rebirth, he experienced a profound transformation of his spirit with unconditional love.

Beckwith's discerning eye went beyond the surface of his troubled past; he saw the potential for positive change within himself. The dream catalyzed transformation, prompting him to shed destructive habits and embrace his spirituality. The power of discernment allowed him to recognize the latent goodness within, leading to a remarkable shift in his life trajectory.

The story of Beckwith illustrates that a discerning eye not only perceives external realities but also unveils the hidden wisdom within oneself. The intuitive insight derived from spiritual discernment becomes a source of motivation, encouraging leaders to overcome challenges and strive for personal and collective betterment.

In the spirit-full leader's narrative, the discerning eye doesn't merely identify talent in others but also recognizes the untapped potential within oneself. Beckwith's journey from a self-proclaimed non-believer and drug dealer to a beacon of love and encouragement showcases the transformative power of intuitive perception. His awakening was a realization that he was more than flesh, mind, and bone—a recognition of the profound spiritual dimension within.

Spirit-full leaders, inspired by their discerning eye, navigate their paths with a deep sense of purpose. Beckwith's commitment to serving the love and beauty of the world reflects the transformative impact of spiritual discernment on leadership. The discerning eye becomes a guiding light, enabling leaders to see beyond immediate challenges, anticipate positive transformations, and trust the inherent goodness that propels them on the right path.

In essence, the discerning eye of a spirit-full leader is a conduit for insights and wisdom that go beyond the visible, tapping into the universal energy that connects all living beings. Through this intuitive perception, spirit-full leaders gain a profound understanding of the world and inspire transformative change within themselves and others.

The discerning eye, guided by spiritual principles, becomes a compass that leads spirit-full leaders to embody the change they wish to see, encouraging a journey of self-discovery, wisdom cultivation, and the pursuit of a higher purpose.

"I believe that you're great, that there's something
magnificent about you. Regardless of what has happened
to you in your life, regardless of how young or old you think you
might be, the moment you begin to think properly, there's
something within you that's greater than the world.
It will begin to emerge. It will take over your life.
It will feed you. It will clothe you. It will guide,
protect, direct, and sustain your existence if you let it.
Now, that is what I know for sure."
~ Michael Beckwith

"Brave leaders are never silent around hard things."

~ Brene Brown

Vulnerability and Sensitivity

L ike humility, vulnerability is often considered a weakness when, in reality, it's a great strength. Vulnerability is a thing of joy, love, and authenticity. When we are vulnerable, we allow ourselves to be seen for who we are. We put ourselves out there and focus on being authentic rather than trying to please others.

Being vulnerable takes courage. It makes us bold and more resilient as we learn to process our emotions effectively and push away the negative ones. So, vulnerability should be embraced instead of fought, as it fosters good mental and emotional health.

This brings us to the teachings of Yasmin Mogahed, who delivered lessons about vulnerability, love, relationships, and spirituality. An Egyptian-born American woman with a psychology degree, Mogahed noticed that her culture focused too much on rituals and the technicalities of her religion and not enough on the spiritual aspects. God was not seen as related to relationships, and vulnerability was regarded as a weakness, especially for Muslim women.

Mogahed powered through the discrimination she experienced and made her perspective heard. This realization that Islam's spirituality was no longer focused on what she believed it should be sparked a new awakening in her spirituality – one where vulnerability keeps your heart true, soft, and full of love.

"Showing vulnerability isn't a weakness. It's a strength. Keep the heart soft. Be unafraid of the creation. Be real with God, yourself, and others. And give. Give out of compassion, knowing that we're all vulnerable. We're all struggling. There's much pain in this world. But there's also so much beauty. Let the pain prepare you for the beauty."
~ Yasmin Mogahed

Sensitivity transcends ordinary perception when elevated to spiritual intelligence. Through heightened sensitivity, spirit-full leaders access a higher consciousness that goes beyond the limitations of the material world. This spiritual intelligence becomes a wellspring of profound insights and wisdom, guiding leaders in their decision-making and shaping a leadership approach that transcends the ordinary.

- In the intricacies of spirit-full leadership, sensitivity emerges as a thread that weaves together self-awareness, empathy, interconnectedness, and spiritual intelligence. Culturing wisdom and insights is delicately linked to the depth of sensitivity leaders bring to their roles.

  By embracing sensitivity, spirit-full leaders navigate the complexities of leadership with grace, foster authentic connections, and contribute to a collective pool of wisdom that transcends individual perspectives. Sensitivity becomes a skill and a way of being—a profound journey transforming leadership into a holistic and enlightened endeavor.

"A leader is best when people barely know he exists, when his work is done, his aim fulfilled, they will say: we did it ourselves."

~ Lao Tzu

AUTHOR BIOGRAPHIES

S tefan Almér is a visionary leader, a seasoned consultant, and a beacon of inspiration in the world of business and personal development.

With his upbringing in the countryside of Sweden, deeply rooted in nature, he grew up with no aspiration to become a leader but curiosity from a voice inside to discover more of his own potential.

Forty years later, through several life experiences and leadership roles, He is a seasoned leader with a passion for transformation and empowering teams to reach new heights. With over two decades of experience in leadership and consulting and a background spanning various leadership roles, including Head of Marketing and Business Development, Head of Human Resources, and Chief Information Officer, Stefan has amassed extensive experience in organizational transformation and strategic development both in the private and public sector.

Stefan's journey into leadership began with a deep-rooted curiosity for understanding human behavior and organizational dynamics. Armed with a passion for making a difference, he embarked on a quest to explore the intersection of spirituality, leadership, and business.

His expertise lies in the depth of understanding how to support people and organizations unfolding the true hidden essence of heart-centered leadership and being as a person and bringing these two together to reveal the hidden potential of the self and the organization.

Drawing upon his rich professional experience and spiritual journey, Stefan's experience is diverse, from business innovation and leadership to energy work, personal development, and frequency guidance. He holds a degree in innovation engineering and have deepened his knowledge of people with multiple leadership courses. He holds a diploma in psychosynthesis therapy and have extensive training in energy work and mental training.

Stefan is known for his warm demeanor, genuine passion for supporting others, and dedication to personal development. As a trusted advisor and coach, Stefan specializes in fostering sustainable culture in today's dynamic business landscape.

Stefans deepest passion is that of discovering new perspectives, way's that go beyond the existing paradigms to reach the unknown.

You can read more about Stefan at www.stayfundevelopment.se

John Spender is a 37-time International best-selling co-author who hadn't learned how to read and write at a basic level until he was ten. He has since traveled to more than 70 countries and territories and started many businesses, leading him to create the best-selling book series *A Journey Of Riches*. He is an award-winning international speaker and movie maker.

John has worked as an international NLP trainer and coached thousands of people from various backgrounds through many challenges. From the borderline homeless to wealthy individuals, he has helped many people connect with their truth to create a life on their terms.

John's search for answers to living a fulfilling life has taken him to work with Native American Indians in the Hills of San Diego, visit the forests of Madagascar, swim with humpback whales in Tonga, explore the Okavango Delta of Botswana, and climb the Great Wall of China. He's traveled from Chile to Slovakia, Hungary to the Solomon Islands, the mountains of Italy, and the streets of Mexico.

Everywhere his journey has taken him, John has discovered a hunger among people to find a new way to live, with a yearning for freedom of expression. His belief that everyone has a book in them was born.

He is now a writing coach, working with over 400 authors from 40 countries for the *A Journey of Riches* series (http:// ajourneyofriches.com/). His publishing house, Motion Media International, publishes non-fiction books.

John also co-wrote and produced the movie documentary *Adversity*, which will be released in 2024 and star Jack Canfield, Rev. Michael Bernard Beckwith, Dr. John Demartini, and many more. You can bet there will be a best-selling book to follow!

AFTERWORD

A s we end this journey through the pages of *Spirit-full Leadership: Discovering Your Inner Guide to Inspire and Lead*, we hope you've found illumination, inspiration, and perhaps a few moments of introspection along the way.

Throughout this book, we have shared insights, anecdotes, and practical guidance from our collective leadership and spirituality experiences. We've invited you to embark on a voyage of self-discovery and urged you to tap into the wellspring of wisdom within each of us.

At the heart of *Spirit-full Leadership* lies the profound notion that effective leadership is not merely about external strategies or techniques but rather about aligning oneself with a deeper, inner wisdom. This intuitive compass guides one's actions and decisions with clarity, authenticity, and purpose.

In a world characterized by chaos, uncertainty, and rapid change, the need for such spirit-full leadership has never been more pressing. Leaders who operate from a deep authenticity and connection with their inner selves are better equipped to navigate the complexities of modern-day challenges. They inspire trust, foster collaboration, and cultivate environments where individuals can flourish and achieve collective goals.

Yet, embracing spirit-full leadership is not always easy. It requires courage—the courage to look within, confront one's fears and limitations, and embrace vulnerability. It demands patience—the patience to listen to the whispers of intuition amidst the cacophony of external voices. Above all, it calls for commitment—the commitment to continually cultivate and nurture the inner guide that serves as a beacon of light on the leadership path.

As you close this book and reflect on its teachings, we encourage you to carry forward the spirit of inquiry and exploration it embodies. Take the time to listen to the still, small voice within you. Trust in its wisdom, and allow it to guide you as you navigate the complexities of leadership and life.

May you embark on your own journey of spirit-full leadership with courage, patience, and unwavering commitment. May the insights shared within these pages inspire and guide you along the way.

With warmest regards,
John & Stefan